Programming in the
Primary Grades

Programming in the Primary Grades

Beyond the Hour of Code

Sam Patterson

ROWMAN & LITTLEFIELD
Lanham • Boulder • New York • London

Published by Rowman & Littlefield International, Ltd.
Unit A, Whitacre Mews, 26–34 Stannary Street, London SE11 4AB
www.rowmaninternational.com

Rowman & Littlefield International, Ltd. is an affiliate of Rowman & Littlefield
4501 Forbes Boulevard, Suite 200, Lanham, Maryland 20706, USA
With additional offices in Boulder, New York, Toronto (Canada), and Plymouth (UK)
www.rowman.com

British Library Cataloguing in Publication Data

Library of Congress Cataloging-in-Publication Data

Names: Patterson, Sam, author.
Title: Programming in the primary grades : beyond the hour of code / Sam Patterson.
Description: Lanham, Maryland : Rowman & Littlefield, 2016. | Includes bibliographical
   references and index.
Identifiers: LCCN 2015046138 (print) | LCCN 2016005893 (ebook) |
   ISBN 9781475825435 (cloth : alk. paper) | ISBN 9781475825442 (pbk. : alk. paper) |
   ISBN 9781475825459 (Electronic)
Subjects: LCSH: Education, Primary—Computer-assisted instruction. |
   Computer programming—Study and teaching (Primary)
Classification: LCC LB1028.5 .P327 2016 (print) | LCC LB1028.5 (ebook) |
   DDC 372.133/4—dc23
LC record available at http://lccn.loc.gov/2015046138

♾™ The paper used in this publication meets the minimum requirements of American
National Standard for Information Sciences—Permanence of Paper for Printed Library
Materials, ANSI/NISO Z39.48-1992.

Printed in the United States of America

Contents

Foreword

As one of the early programmers of the Apple II computer, and the first to write a book on how to program the Apple II in assembly language, I have a deep appreciation of the benefits of learning to code. When I began my own journey of discovery with computers, the only way to make the computer do what you imagined it could do was to yourself write the direct instructions that would make it do just that thing.

One of the great benefits when anyone, and in particular a young person, begins that journey for themselves is the discovery of exactly how the technology now around us everywhere actually does what it does. That for any task done by a computing device, whether it be a laptop, a mobile phone, or a quadcopter drone, at the heart of it all is code running something, written by a living person that imagined that process, and then brought it into being by writing the words and phrasing on a computer screen that made their imagination manifest.

As students take on the challenge of crafting their own programs that will give form to their imagination, they will also learn—in fact cannot escape the learning, of patience and persistence and attention to detail. They will learn the concepts of flow, sequence, and conditional branching, along with mathematical operations, and that the design of the functions creates the outcome.

The computer processing the instructions of a program is immovable in its insistence of following exactly what the programmer has constructed, and when the instructions are incomplete or malformed, the end result just isn't achieved. There is a pragmatic achievement of goals, where as we say, "crying won't make your program work."

Along the way, they will also learn about the importance of the quality of workmanship. A program that "almost works" often just doesn't work at all. Perfection is difficult to achieve, but the pursuit of it is a worthy challenge, achieved through the aforementioned patience, persistence, and attention to detail. Quality coding is an art form in itself, and recognized both academically and professionally.

One of my personal sayings is, "clear in language, clear in thought," and nowhere is that more true than in coding. It is just not possible to write a computer program without having thought through what each line of the program is doing in its part toward the ultimate objective of the purpose of the program.

One does not learn these skills and benefit from the experience in just an hour, any more than writing a single poem in an hour in first grade would be a sufficient experience in writing and literature. The Hour of Code is intended to be the first introduction, the "aha! moment" for a student to realize that the computer *can* be controlled by what they write, and that they can be more than just consumers of technology. That they can actively control what is unquestionably the most powerful force in today's world.

It is what happens next after opening that door that Sam Patterson's book gives wings to. This book will help teachers at all levels of experience and confidence and is written by an experienced educator, reaching out to other elementary educators to help them use programming in a meaningful way.

The text assures teachers that they don't have to be a programmer to teach programming, by leveraging the use of classroom-ready tools currently available that are designed to provide a low threshold to entry while still delivering high-engagement teaching. Sam Patterson's years of unique experience in the classroom with mathematics, robotics, literature, photography, and makerspaces will give you a perspective and working strategy to ensure your success as you introduce your students to the concepts of programming.

Congratulations on taking this next step beyond the Hour of Code to bring to your students the many gifts offered by exploring the world of programming and coding!

Roger Wagner

Roger Wagner
Creator and Designer, HyperStudio
Inventor of the HyperDuino
Author of *Assembly Lines: The Book*, the first book on
how to program the Apple II in assembly language-1981

Preface

Thank you for joining me on this journey. When I began teaching elementary technology class three years ago, I was really lucky to join a team of awesome teachers. Together, we have been figuring out the best uses for technology and programming in grades K-5. At the beginning, none of us knew anything about programming.

If you are willing to learn as you go, there are many amazing things programming in class can make available to you. As you read this text, think about how this could work in your context.

What lessons do you need to make more engaging? Where is your learning stopping before it gets to the more conceptual level? These are the problems you should have in the back of your mind as you read this text.

When we build amazing learning experiences and set appropriate goals, our students can learn an incredible amount about the world and themselves, as they play in class.

Author's Note

This book is designed to get teachers energized and empowered to use programming as a mode of instruction outside of technology class. Grade level teachers working with a technology coach developed the lessons described in this book. The tips and tricks come straight out of their classrooms.

The first chapters make the argument for programming as a mode of learning, and then the book really begins to describe specific lessons and modes of programming. Chapters three through seven are a survey of popular programming platforms and a discussion of the learning they support.

The final third of the book is dedicated to discussing what programming to learn looks like for lessons focusing on social skills, STEM learning, and literacy.

Chapter 1

Why Teach Programming in the Primary Grades?

The nature of technological revolution and advancement is that new tools can profoundly change the world. As teachers, the challenge we face is to prepare our students to be contributing members of a society that does not yet exist.

Consider the shift in manufacturing in the last fifty years. As we developed more efficient ways to ship and track goods, jobs moved to where the labor was cheaper than the difference in transportation cost. During the same time, education changed very little. Schools were developed to prepare students for the workplace. Bells signaled when classes began, and compliance was rewarded. We placed a great emphasis on correctness and timeliness. These were the values that would make manufacturing efficient.

Now we know that we have missed the mark for prepping students for the jobs needed in the twenty-first century. There are plenty of sources out there that can point to how many computer science workers we need and how few we have. For example, Code.org shares the statistic that computer science jobs are growing at twice the national average; by 2020 there will be one million more computer science jobs than there are students.

While the key qualities of a manufacturing worker were timeliness, efficiency, and compliance, the qualities to succeed in today's workplace show a pivot toward independence and problem solving (See Table 1.1).

This pivot toward an economy of information is clear in the first skills. Leading the way for twenty-first century skills are communication and computer skills. Verbal and written communication can be a daily practice in any classroom, and it should be made an important part of daily routine. It is not hard to support this—start by asking students to make decisions in pairs or small groups. Teachers can write directions and messages to students and then

Table 1.1　Twenty-First Century Skills Pivot

Twentieth Century Skills	*Twenty-first Century Skills**
Rote Mastery of Facts	**Content Knowledge and Twenty-first Century Themes** – Global awareness – Financial, economic, business, and entrepreneurial literacy – Civic literacy – Health literacy – Environmental literacy
Compliance and Timeliness	**Learning and Innovation Skills** – Creativity and innovation – Critical thinking and problem solving – Communication and collaboration
Basic Literacy	**Information, Media, and Technology Skills** – Information literacy – Media literacy – ICT literacy
Community Involvement	**Life and Career Skills** – Flexibility and adaptability – Initiative and self-direction – Social and cross-cultural skills – Productivity and accountability – Leadership and responsibility

*From the Partnership for Twenty-first Century Skills, www.p21.org.

ask the students to read them. Do not write a message to students and then read it directly to them, for this undercuts the purpose of the written message.

Thinking and problem-solving skills are newer to the scene than communication. Clearly a worker of this century needs to be able to collaborate as well as solve problems. The workers of our century need to see themselves as flexible, because what they do will change significantly over time. The world can change, and has changed, radically, and it will continue to do so. The work of today is responding to challenges with innovation, so the worker of today must have a fluid mindset and think dynamically about resources.

The balance of the ten skills identified by the Partnership for Twentieth Century Skills all focus on interpersonal relations and self-direction. Self-directional skills are the tools students need to succeed in a world where they will often be unmanaged. There will not be bells that ring to initiate the workday, or whistles for the lunch hour. Management might be in a different building, country, or even orbit. Self-confidence and a strong work ethic are very important when working in a remote or distributed network of individuals.

When workers don't share physical space, their interpersonal skills become even more important. Without the ongoing informal contact created by cohabiting the same office, remote workers will need to have the interpersonal skills to maintain satisfying relationships with their coworkers. Honesty and teamwork are essential to the model of work where individuals collaborate with various stakeholders on different projects.

Schools have been growing and adapting to support this skill building. There is an increase in project-based learning, which uses group work and design thinking to address real needs within the school community.

As a teacher, you might have thought about these challenges yourself. As you plan lessons you might have found meaningful ways to have students work together. You might have had them create videos to explain their problem-solving methods. You might have even wondered how computer programming can support these broad educational goals.

Is teaching kids to program the most important work to do in schools and at home? It is not. The mission of this text is not to get every kid programming (that work is being done by computer science teachers everywhere with the support of Code.org and the Computer Science Teachers Organization at http://www.csta.acm.org/) but to connect programming with content-area curriculum. The mission is to help teachers design content-rich lessons that use programming as a means of expression.

Programming is a cognitively complex activity that allows students creator-level access to media they had previously only interacted with as consumers. Past students may have been parked in front of Math Blaster for twenty minutes a week in the name of digital learning. Now we can ask students to *create* games, writing new levels and challenges in a Math-Blaster-style game, and it is within their grasp. Students can learn much more building an edtech game than playing one.

Teachers already have a toolbox packed with strategies to help kids share their developing understandings of concepts and relationships. Students are asked to verbally respond to questions, write about what they understand, or move around to show that they comprehend the sequence of a series of movements. When we ask students to apply their understanding, they sometimes draw a picture, write a poem, build a diorama, or make a movie.

Mobile computing, from tablets to Chromebooks, has blown up our old instructional toolbox and created a world of pedagogical possibilities. With some devices costing less than $200, the tools are available to have every student create their own movie or animation. Teachers can craft digital learning experiences that encourage children to program their understanding into an interactive text or game. Teachers and students can use programming to demonstrate as well as develop content-area understanding.

WHY TEACH PROGRAMMING IN THE PRIMARY GRADE?

One of the many joys of teaching elementary school is that you can teach so many different things in a naturally integrated way. You can teach science through songs and math through art. You can even teach reading through storytelling. So why is it important to dedicate time to programming?

In many ways, despite the career-based arguments, computer programming in elementary grades is not about programming. When we design meaningful digital learning experiences for our students, we are not doing it because we want them all to learn to code.

When teachers choose to make programming a vehicle for learning, they are setting a stage for education that reaches far beyond computer-science-related learning objectives. In a well-constructed lesson, you can teach social skills as students work together programming a robot to select the solution to a math challenge. Students can be immersed in problem solving, while working together to figure out what they could not master alone.

Resilience and the willingness to try again are also excellent learning goals for a programming lesson. This text is full of lessons that layer these affective learning objectives on top of the more concrete content-area learning objectives. The lessons highlight how other teachers have taken lessons they have used for years and strategically added some aspect of programming in order to amplify and multiply the learning achieved.

Programming Is Expressive

This may come as a surprise to you, but computer programming is a means of expression. When students are asked to create a game in the tradition of "Oregon Trail," they are, in fact, asked to apply their understanding of history. In the process of crafting the game experience, the students show what they understand about the time period, and they reveal what seems most important to them. The game becomes a text wherein the author interacts with the reader.

If you ask students to create an animated coral reef, they have the opportunity to use the knowledge studied in class to bring a coral reef to life. The coral reef created is a unique documenting of their understanding of the reef filtered through their understanding of programming. A short code talk—having the students share their goals, process, and compromises—can shed a great deal of light on where the programming-understanding limited the student's ability to relate her science-understanding.

First You Learn to Code, Then You Learn Through Code

Mitch Resnick, the researcher who developed Scratch, describes programming as a medium of learning and comprehension building. When students are asked to program fish to swim in a coral reef, they are going to ask how a starfish swims. They will wonder if a whale belongs in the reef. They will ask the other students in their table group what color they should make the seahorse. Students will get the books off the shelf and look up the images and stories the class has shared in order to make an accurate model. Programming this challenge instead of making a poster allows the students to move past the simple question of "What is it?" to more advanced questions like "What does it do?" and "How does it relate to the rest of the environment?"

Programming is a vehicle teachers can use to help students develop a more complete understanding of any subject. At its most integrated, programming becomes another way we have students process information. In the youngest grades, programming slows them down enough to enforce procedural thinking.

Programming and the Three Rs

Reading: As we dive deep into how programming can be used to support subject area learning, we will look at research that shows how the sequencing that students do in game-style programming apps can positively impact their growing literacy skills. Even when students are not doing content-specific meaning making through programming, they are developing fundamental learning and literacy skills.

Writing: It is useful to think of a video game as an interactive story. The text is written in full before it ever goes to market, but the audience controls much of how the story unfolds, similar to the old-school choose-your-own-adventure books. When we ask students to create a game in a programming app, they have to build a narrative for the player. The author has to have a clear sense of the beginning, middle, and end of the game. In more complex games, the author has to have a sense of these three sections for the overall game as well as each level.

Arithmetic: Programming is a playground of applied mathematics. The first curricular uses of programming happened in math classes using Logo, created by Cynthia Solomon, Wally Feurzeig, and Seymour Parapet in 1967. From the basic number line math needed to figure out how many spaces a character needs to move, to the qualities of regular polygons, programming asks us to apply mathematical understanding constantly. With guidance, even our youngest students can use a programming challenge to build numeracy skills.

As students become more skilled, they can use math more actively in their programs. From counting, to geometry, to variables, to order of operations, programming provides so many opportunities to make abstract learning concrete by applying it to a character or a programming challenge.

Programming and Common Core Math

"In the new approach, as you know, the important thing is to understand what you are doing, rather than get the right answer." Tom Lehrer's laugh line from the 1965 song "New Math" could easily describe the current discussion around math. Teachers who care about a deep understanding of mathematics have been arguing for decades that the focus of math instruction should not be computation. The Common Core standards are the most recent episode in the slowly evolving approach to math instruction.

The challenge to teachers is that although they want students to understand the operational math behind the individual problems, the only tools the math teachers have are books full of math problems. Math problems beg solving. Solving a problem feels final. Nothing says closure like an equals sign or a bottom line. That is the nature of a math problem, and nothing is going to change that.

Programming is a perfect answer to this quandary. Programming removes the student from the computational role. The student now has to design a program that can manage the computation. Programming a problem solver focuses the student on how the mathematical operation works. They have to break the operation down into discrete actions and program the app to undergo those actions in the correct sequence. The program is a literal codification of the operation.

A student engaged in writing the problem solver, individually or as part of a group, has a focus far beyond the individual digits she is using to test her program. Programming has shifted this student's work and thought to another level. Finding the solution to a hundred problems will not yield the same understanding as writing a program to solve those same problems.

Where to Begin?

Let's begin with this promise: you can find a programming platform that will help you learn alongside your students. The platform will have built-in tutorials as well as a curriculum guide. The platform will work with the tech you have right now.

This book will explain all of the platforms available and help teachers develop their own sequence of activities and skills that move students from leveled apps into content-area lessons in open studio apps. By the end of this book, teachers should have a good understanding of several basic types of programming-based content-area lessons and their own list of ready-to-roll lessons to support learning.

The multigrade focus of the text is designed to help teachers see how programming skills build year over year. It can also help teachers develop an understanding of how programming skills are applied to content-area learning and how that changes from one year of instruction to the next.

Just like reading, writing, and math, once teachers see how this knowledge and practice builds over years, they can release themselves of the responsibility of teaching "all" of programming.

Chapter 2

What Can We Learn Through Programming?

What can we learn through programming? It is a question of potential and possibility, a challenge to the imagination of the teacher as well as the learner. As noted in chapter 1, Mitch Resnick, creator of the Scratch programming language, has said that first we learn to program and then we learn through programming. But what does it mean to learn through programming?

The learning goals we set in a coding lesson can and should transcend computer science skills, computational thinking, and programming concepts. In a well-constructed lesson that uses programming, teachers can meet standards in almost any subject area. In this chapter, we will explore the role programming can play in building and assessing student skills over a range of subjects, and, in later chapters, we will dive deep into specific lessons focusing on social and emotional learning, literacy, math, and science.

PROGRAMMING IS COMMUNICATION

When a team of software developers creates an app, whether a fitness tracking app or something that turns your lights on as soon as you pull into the driveway, they have written a text. In the broadest sense, these programs are a text created by authors that the audience interacts with. When they are writing these texts, they share them with test or beta audiences and adjust the program to make sure that the audience can use it as designed.

Just like a newspaper article, a movie script, or a pictograph-style set of furniture assembly instructions, computer programs are written to translate the author's intention to the audience. A computer program is a communication between two people.

Students are asked to communicate their understanding in many ways every day in class. We have them write dialogues between characters, create presentations, build dioramas, write reports, and make movies. Each one of these boilerplate school texts can be adapted to incorporate programming. When teachers learn how to use programming as a mode of instruction, they add another powerful tool to their lesson design toolbox.

Applied Problem Solving

Programming to craft a text, whether it is an interactive game or a short movie-style animation, requires students to set a goal and work to meet it. As they work between their idea of what they want the program to do and what it is currently doing, they are actively problem solving. Borrowing from the world of writing instruction, we could call this revision, but it is different. When crafting writing, almost all people need to show the text to someone else to get their perspective on whether or not it works. With programming, the problems show up front and center, and students can try multiple solutions without waiting on another person to give them feedback.

Initially students will claim that the program is broken, or the app is "glitching." Almost all the time, if someone else carefully reads through the programming with the student, the error can be located and corrected. Soon students come to understand the app or the robot is following the directions given. They try giving different directions, and if that does not work, they have to try another strategy.

Often in a class using programming, a teacher does not have a complete knowledge of the language or platform being used. Students exploring the platform to find a solution to their problem may discover something the instructor did not know is possible. It is not uncommon to have students significantly improve the starter program teachers give them as they figure out a better way to meet the challenge.

The reality of this might make some teachers nervous. There are very few teachers who would claim that they got into education so they could lead a room full of students through something they do not fully understand. This is the situation we find ourselves in, as the tools available to us are changing everyday. While it might not be the most comfortable position for a teacher, this is a golden opportunity.

John Dewey, writing in 1920, imagined a system of education that put the student at the center, with hands-on learning empowering students to be creators of knowledge. This is what is possible when we take the risk of changing the instructional role of the teacher. When we design learning experiences that ask students to create, problem solve, discover, and collaborate, we create the conditions where students can own the knowledge they produce instead of merely following directions.

What can students learn through programming in class? They can learn that they have the ability to figure something out. They can learn that they can be helpful to others. And, most importantly, they can learn that everyone in the room has something to contribute to the class knowledge base. The students that emerge as skilled leaders in programming are often different than those that rise to the top in traditional reading- and writing-focused lessons.

To the Standards and Beyond!

When we program to learn and design digital learning experiences that ask students to use programming to create meaningful texts with core subject content, we ask the students to apply content-area knowledge in a complex and engaging environment.

Two students in second grade using ScratchJr to create a dialogue between a beekeeper and a bee have to manage multiple challenges. There is the challenge of programming the script pieces to appear in the right order, and there is also the challenge of what each character will say. There are also choices to make about where the characters are conversing. So this programming lesson becomes an extended conversation about the science content the class has recently covered. Often students use notes, worksheets, and science journals as source material while they create their short animation.

Computer Science

Although it seems obvious, it bears mentioning: programming in class can help students learn the fundamentals of programming and computational thinking. Even the simplest programming activity can help students understand basic syntax, sequence, and the relationship between input and output. As the programming tasks get more complex, so do the programming tools and concepts. Students will learn how loops and repetition can make a program shorter and more elegant. They will learn how to group commands into a function that they can use at any point in the program. Once they start working with robots, students will learn how to use input from sensors to trigger events in the program.

Collaboration

Programming in class can foster collaboration because much of the time students need to help each other to figure out how to finish a level in Kodable, or how to get Scratch the cat to dance perfectly. Even when students are working on their own devices, many teachers use the rule "Ask three then me" to support collaboration. (If students have a problem, they have to ask three classmates before going to the teacher for help.) From the perspective of the teacher, this has two purposes. The first is that students look to each other for help. This is important because many times as a subject area teacher using programming, some students in the room might have more hands-on experience and knowledge of the programming platform.

The second purpose to using "Ask three then me" is that it keeps the work moving. If the teacher tries to answer all the questions in the room, students will stop learning as soon as they raise their hand and begin waiting. Training your students to use each other as a resource keeps them actively involved in problem solving. When students are talking with each other about a problem, they are both learning. When a student has a hand raised, staring at the busy teacher and waiting for help, the learning has stopped. The classroom is not a theme park; no one should be waiting in line to learn.

Content-Area Knowledge

This is the biggest reason for the text in your hand right now. Teachers can design meaningful lessons that use programming to help students master content-area knowledge. Math provides a simple example. If you present students with a math problem, they will often blurt out an answer before you have even asked them to solve it. Teachers are always looking for ways to interrupt this rush to computation and get students to engage with the content. What if, instead of asking students to solve problems, students were asked to write a program that solves the problem?

When students have to write a program to solve a math problem, they must get to the point where they understand exactly what the problem is asking them to do. Once their program solves one problem, can it solve a related problem? As the students share the program they are writing, they provide more data about their understanding than simply whether or not they arrived at the correct solution.

If you are learning about a process, for example, photosynthesis, students can use programming to create an animation that shows photosynthesis in action. When students use programming to create a model of a process, they have to understand the process very well. Assessment is simple: watch the animation and see if it works. Students are challenged to build a model with moving and interacting parts. Copying the work of the student next to you is not practical when everything on the screen has its own program attached to it.

Learning to spell? You can use programming to add a layer of sequencing to lessons on sight words. Kindergarten students can program jumbled letters into their correct positions on a line using ScratchJr. First and second grade students can build their own vocabulary and spelling games using ScratchJr and Hopscotch. Once your students see the games and lessons you can build in open studio apps, they will want to build their own and share them with each other. When was the last time that happened with a worksheet?

Voice

A computer program is a text. The author constructed it with an idea in mind, a purpose. The reader or audience experiences the program and gains their own understanding of the message constructed by the author. When students participate in this type of creative exchange, it helps them develop a sense of themselves. In English class, we might call this a writer's voice.

Fundamentally, voice is the knowledge that the text you create is different than the text someone else would create. When we set meaningful challenges for students and leave them plenty of room to make meaningful choices, the work they create can be uniquely their own. If this type of creative, expressive activity is a regular feature of learning in your class, students will develop a stronger sense of personal identity, and they will feel more empowered in their learning. By asking your students to share their understanding through programming, you give them the chance to see that their understanding is their own. In turn they will develop a strong sense of ownership of this knowledge. They will learn that they have something to share with the world.

How to Learn

Learning anything through programming is going to have challenges. As your students work with you and their peers, they will have many chances to learn about themselves as learners. Often you might find that the appropriate teacher role is to ask students to place the tablets face down and share something they notice or wonder. A brief popcorn share can help students get insight into what other students are doing, as well as allowing students to see that they are not alone in their frustration. In a popcorn share, students are asked to share what they have noticed while working, students share freely without raising of hands. Failure is part of the process, and some of the most active work teachers do in a programming classroom is engaging students who are trying to figure out what to try next.

Over time, your students will develop problem-solving protocols as well as their own understanding of which resources work best for them. Some students will find YouTube videos helpful, while others will discover that they need to observe a classmate in order to figure out how to do something. Metacognition, individually and in small- and whole-group settings, can help students see how others overcome challenges and solve problems. This builds their personal resource bank for the next time they get stuck.

WHAT THE CONTEXT OF PROGRAMMING AFFORDS

Programming is a flexible medium for learning. There are many tools and platforms that can be used, many goals that can be met. This alone does not define the educational value of programming. When students work together to program a robot or design an app, there is a uniquely charged collaborative process. Charged because the tech tools often carry a very high level of engagement, thus creating interpersonal challenges as well as opportunities.

Teachers can use programming to make something as simple as a review of morning meeting protocol into a cognitively complex group project to write a morning meeting program. This uses the engagement of programming to power the review of protocol. Students will also remember it better because they were actively deconstructing the protocol while creating the program. When a protocol changes, students could draft a new program to reflect the change. If the program is visible to all the students, it can be changed every morning and students would still be able to do the right thing.

Programming is a pedagogical tool that creates situations for deeper cognition, parallel repetition, and novel performance-based group interaction.

Deeper Cognition

Deeper cognition comes from changing the relationship between the student and the challenge. When we ask students to create a program to solve a math problem, we remove them from the role of computation and place the program they create in that role instead. We have asked the student to write a program that will compute. The student is focused on conceptual understanding of the math, not solving one problem.

Parallel Repetition

Parallel repetition happens when we ask students to sequence about sequence. For example, first grade students use Bee-Bots to study the planets. They program the robots to navigate from the first planet to the second and then on to the third until they reach the edge of the solar system (which does or does not mention Pluto, depending on which of the books in the room you are reading). Working in small groups of four, the students are going over the order of planets again and again. They are programming the bot to move from the first to the second. As their fellow group members program, the onlookers debug and predict problems. They may suggest solutions.

Novel Performance-Based Group Interaction

In this case, "novel" means unique. Programming calls on different skills and resources than many other activities in the classroom. The students who struggle with reading and math lessons may be top problem solvers in a programming class. Teachers often find that the students who struggle in other aspects of class find themselves empowered by their knowledge and understanding when the class is programming. Giving these students an opportunity to be empowered can change everything.

Many students struggle to feel successful and be a part of the class culture. When a student discovers something in a programming app and shares it with other students, there is a sense of purpose and recognition. Programming requires community. Programming languages change and come into being constantly; no one person can know everything. As students learn about programming, they will read tutorials, and, when they figure out something on their own, they will want to write a tutorial or make a screen cast.

Programming affords us the opportunity to empower students who may feel unconnected to a textbook or uninspired by a sheet of proofs. Programming gives students tangible complex challenges to address.

Chapter 3

Off-line Programming and the Power of Dance to Develop Logic

One of the most often touted benefits of introducing students to programming is that it helps them develop "computational thinking." Unfortunately, this is often presented as though it is a universally accepted concept, but it is not. To most teachers this sounds like a vague dodge of the question, "What standards are addressed?"

What Is Computational Thinking?

There is a great and detailed discussion of computational thinking at http://scratched.gse.harvard.edu/ct/defining.html. By studying the work done in the online Scratch community, Harvard researchers observed three key dimensions of computational thinking: "(1) computational concepts, (2) computational practices, and (3) computational perspectives."

Concepts include key ideas and commands occurring in many programming and nonprogramming contexts, including sequences, loops, conditionals, and others. Practices are the routines programmers engage in, such as experimenting, iterating, testing, and remixing.

Perspectives focus on the changing habits of the mind of programmers. These include realizing that programming is an act of creation, discovering that working with others can yield different results, and feeling empowered to ask questions about the world.

Why Program Off-line?

When we approach teaching computational thinking mindfully and with intention, we strive to have the student experience important concepts, practices, and perspectives in a variety of contexts. If we only wanted our students

17

thinking about programming when they are on a tablet, then we will only talk about algorithms and programs when the students are holding tablets. If we want to help our students create a flexible and dynamic schema for programming, we will find a variety of connected and unconnected contexts to practice computational thinking.

Programming without devices, also referred to as off-line or unplugged programming, is fun for kids and helps them focus on the programming *concept* rather than the programming medium. When we take the time to guide students through learning experiences that highlight the same concepts in vastly different contexts, students develop a more complete and flexible understanding of those concepts. For example, a second grader learning about squares might draw squares, engage with math aids that are squares, take picture of squares, program Hopscotch to create squares, and program a robot to draw a square on paper. These ideas can move from a skill, which is very context centered, to deeper knowledge. This shift is empowering the students; this empowerment is one of our highest goals. We want students to understand what they are learning so deeply it becomes part of how they see themselves.

Movement is good for everybody. Off-line programming can be done in any space, and it gets kids up and moving. Students need to move throughout the day, and regular short physical periods support learning and improve their ability to focus. Programming can be used as the lesson structure for an activity about how to sort the recycling or dance the "Dougie." Once the class has a set programming language, you can put a program on the front screen and allow them to figure it out. Once they have a sense of the steps in the dance, turn the music on.

There are great resources available for unplugged programming, many of which have been developed by teachers trying to meet the challenge of teaching programming without the appropriate technology available. This chapter will discuss two off-line coding activities and how they fit into a sequence of physical education and computer science instruction.

While there are full unplugged K-12 curricula for off-line programming, like http://csunplugged.org/, the focus of this chapter is adapting off-line programming as an instructional tool for core content-area learning.

What Are the Components of a Good Off-line Programming Lesson?

1. Use a programming concept and make it visible. When you are working on learning about sequence in programming, have the students build small sequences of steps to create a dance. When the students work, they should always have a written version of their program to refer to. Programming cards or even playing cards can work well for the youngest students.

2. Use the vocabulary you have introduced in your programming lessons in the off-line lessons as well. Once you refer to a series of commands as an algorithm, continue to use the word in all appropriate contexts. Use new terms bravely and invite students to do so as well. There are resources for computer science vocabulary and concepts in the last chapter.

3. Use the physical space. One of the great joys of off-line programing is that it can get kids moving. Look for squares on the ground and then use these as units in the program. So "Forward 1" could mean move forward one square. When we can make connections between our desktops and the real world, students are naturally interested. Can they write a program that moves them from their desk to the door? Where does your class go in a day? Can you write a program to the water fountain? How about the music room?

Getting Started with the Fuzz Family Frenzy

The team at Kodable put together a great forty-five to sixty-minute lesson that gets kids coding and working with programming concepts as well as practices. The two-page handout is available at https://www.kodable.com/resources. The basic idea is to pair students, with one student as the robot and the other as the programmer. The programmer has to write code to get the robot through a simple obstacle course. The code is written in simple arrow-based commands for left leg forward, right leg forward, left leg back, right leg back, body rotate left, body rotate right, jump, squat, grab, and drop.

In the lesson, the teacher introduces the code and runs a very brief example. A note here on examples: start by underexplaining the task at hand. Although it runs counter to a great deal of teacher training, in order to leave room for discovery and accomplishment, we have to avoid providing students with the solution. The programmers need to understand how to write the code and the robots need to understand that they can only do what the code says.

This lesson also works well with groups of three students. With a group of three, two write the program and one is the robot. Plan enough time for everyone to get to be the robot, and encourage funny robot noises. Funny robot noises are very important—in fact, you might suggest the students create a code for funny noises. The teacher could then write a conditional statement, "If I raise my hand, all robot noises stop."

In the realm of computational thinking, this activity gets kids writing directions and watching a robot follow those directions exactly. Keep the obstacle course simple the first time you try this. After the students get the hang of it, this is an activity you may deploy to learn any physical routine or system of movements.

An activity like Fuzz Family Frenzy is a great way to get students thinking about programming without the distraction of a tablet or an actual robot in front of them. As they continue programming and learning, they will practice the same skills they have learned in this activity, with added tablets and robots. Building these skills off-line first means that when you adopt a new platform, students will be able to focus on the new aspects of the lesson and rely on their preexisting basic knowledge of how programming works.

Dances with Robots

Off-line programming is a great tool for introducing concepts, and the lesson above is really the most simple of lessons. It focuses on sequence and command. Let's consider a slightly more advanced concept, the loop. In programming, loops are a set of commands that get repeated in order for a set number of times or until a condition is met. A program might contain a loop that is set to repeat ten times, or a loop that could be set to repeat until the music ends.

When designing an off-line programming lesson about loops, you want to use something fun that is an actual loop. Few things fit the bill as well as dance. Your class may already have dances you do, and, after reading this lesson, you will know exactly how to adapt this idea for the students in your class.

A simple dance that repeats itself a great deal is the Cupid Shuffle. According to a wikiHow page, the Cupid Shuffle has very few steps:

1. Step to the right
   Step to the right
   Step to the right
   Step to the right
2. Step to the left
   Step to the left
   Step to the left
   Step to the left
3. Kick your left leg forward to rest your heel on the ground
4. Kick your right leg forward to rest your heel on the ground
5. Kick your left leg forward to rest your heel on the ground
6. Kick your right leg forward to rest your heel on the ground
7. Walk in place and turn your body 90 degree
8. Return to step one and repeat the entire sequence four times.

This is well suited to teaching loops, because it is a repeated sequence with repeated sequences inside of it. In programming, this is referred to as a nested loop. In the flow of a lesson, begin with all of these instructions on the board, either symbolically for prereaders or written out if your students are all reading.

Without talking about loops, have everybody follow the directions together and do the dance. Then stop and talk about how the directions could be written in a shorter way. Focus just on step one. You should get several ideas from the students about how to write the commands more efficiently. It could be something as simple as "→×4" or "step right four times." This is a simple repeat loop. At this point in the lesson you introduce the word "loop," after they have already discovered the purpose. The purpose of the loop is to write the code more efficiently.

Once the students have been introduced to the loop, have them each work on their own set of instructions for the rest of the dance. You might see which student or team of students can write the shortest code that still works. A fun way to check the code is to have groups exchange code and then all do the dance together. It will be really clear when someone's code isn't working, because they will be out of step.

An activity like dancing loops helps students experience the abstract concept of loops in a very concrete way. You could expand this lesson to include conditionals by adding the command, "As long as the music is playing, repeat this loop." Start and stop the music, and have them use their sound sensors (ears) to detect when the music stops. Could students create different dances for different music?

If your class enjoys brain breaks and dancing, you might have already used the website GoNoodle.com. The site is a great collection of free resources to get kids moving, stretching, and thinking, and it has resources for mindfulness as well. These videos are a great opportunity to inject programming. Students can choose a routine and break it down into a program. This will be more successful if the students can already "do" the dance in the video they are programming for. Once the program is written, the students can share it with other classes. In fact, a great way to illustrate the power of code is to share the code with other classes and arrange a flashmob where everyone dances together in the gym, all made possible by the program.

A lesson like this is easy to build on late in the year, or even in following years. Students can create their own dance and then program an actual robot, like a Sphero or Dash, to be their dancing partner. The trick here is that, like Ginger Rogers, the robot has to do everything backward. It will take the students multiple tries to get the distances dialed in to match their footsteps.

The Special Utility of Programming in Physical Education

With the advent of the Fitbit and the wild proliferation of sensors, we are at the beginning of a wearable tech revolution. In the next decade, the opportunities for meaningful tech integration into physical education will be revolutionized by personal data collection. Even before the wearable tech wave hits the four-square set, there are amazing ways to use computational thinking to help students develop a deeper understanding of what they are doing in physical education.

The Logic of Rules

Students learning the rules of a new game, like pickleball, are well supported by anchoring the discussion of rules in the conditional language of programming. "If the ball lands on the outside of the line, it is out." Writing logic statements about the rules of a game draws the students' attention to the overall system, while giving the rule a context that makes the rules more meaningful.

When we expand our usual discussion on the rules to include an activity where we program about the rules, the students develop a much clearer understanding of the rules. The students do not need devices to do this. They can write logic statements on white boards, papers, or even chalk directly on the asphalt pickleball court if the goal is to contextualize the rules fully. Asking students to write logic statements based on rules of a game adds variety to the routine of introducing games and gives them a chance to study the rules more closely while completing a novel challenge.

The Power of Procedural Thinking

Differentiation can be a real challenge in physical education. Often classes take place outside, and presenting information visually can be almost impossible except for live demonstration. Students can be supported to a deeper understanding of complex physical tasks or routines by translating them into computer-style programs with simple notation. With no more equipment than a journal or paper notebook and pencil, they can break down a series into discrete steps. From performing a cartwheel to participating in a square dance, teachers can use programming to help students think procedurally about a series of actions.

In the example above, the Cupid Shuffle is broken down into steps, and it is a simple dance. Consider the power of using program notation for learning Yoga or Cheerleading. Students could master the moves in one position or subroutine and then connect them into longer sequences. There are plenty of other off-line programming ideas out there, but this chapter focuses on dance because it is really about making programming concepts physical and tangible. The dance lesson is also easily adaptable to fit with any content for which you have a song and choreography available. Consider "Head,

Shoulders, Knees, and Toes" for younger students. The commands could simply be written with stick figures and arrows.

If your students are struggling with an on-screen concept, return to the real world. Use the physical space you are in to help them problem solve. Once you do this a few times as a whole class, you will notice students doing it independently when they need to.

Chapter 4

Programming for Prereaders

Programming fits well into elementary grades because it is a developmentally appropriate complex cognitive task. When students are solving puzzles in The Foos, a leveled text-free programming app, they are building skills needed for reading. The sequencing and planning involved in programming support literacy skill development. Start this chapter by truly believing that children can develop cognitive complexity and logic *before* writing and reading. In fact it is the brain's developing capacity for complex thought and logic that makes reading possible.

Beyond the inherent benefits of programming, teachers can design content-rich digital learning activities using free mobile programming platforms. With the tools currently available, literacy is no longer a gatekeeper to programming. Students who are not yet reading can program applications, robots, and even each other (as robot actors) using off-line programming ideas.

There are many different programming tools and platforms designed specifically for prereaders. You might already be wondering which tools you should support and what the cost will be. Before you make any decisions about the tools, consider the range of ages and skills the tools can support. Does the tool perform a unique function? Is it easy to deploy and store? Most importantly, does the tool support your class values and goals?

The previous chapter discussed some of the potential of off-line programming. This chapter will focus on a range of programming options specifically appropriate for students who are not yet independent readers. Each mode of programming can host different types of learning. Along with each programming platform, sample lessons are discussed and outlined. As we read about these tools, it is important to imagine our students working with them.

Skills That Come with Programming

Even before content learning support is considered, programming as an activity helps students build developmental skills in logic, coordination, and literacy:

- Reading a screen to answer the question, "What does it want me to do?"
- Syntax awareness
- Sequencing
- Understanding the relationship between commands and actions
- Fine motor skills
- Reading code as it is executed

Apps or robots could create conditions for successful literacy skill development. Does this mean we have a green light to hand our children an iPad, set a timer, and call it teaching? Having access to devices requires teachers to constantly rethink their instructional methods.

If student time on tablets is app centered and independent, the technology can be a very disruptive force in the classroom. When students see technology as an individual tool that is disconnected from instruction, some of the worst potentials of tablets are reinforced. Rewarding students with an individual math app makes math app time seem more important than instruction. The lesson is just an obstacle to overcome on the way to independent tech time.

If we use our tech as a reward, as something individual and outside of a genuine instructional context, then this is all students will expect from us. On the other hand, if we use technology to meet challenges and solve problems together, it becomes just another tool we are using to complete the hard fun of learning.

Is that enough? Once you know that there is a fun and engaging tool that develops literacy skills and can be used at the heart of lessons for any content area, what more do you need to know? You can also rest easy in the knowledge that programming in schools is nothing new. Although our current tools have given students previously unheard of access, schools have been teaching programming for a long time.

The Power of Programming

In 1986, it was standard practice to have students programming in school. There was a technology class that had computers, often one for every child. Students would use a simple programming language like LOGO or BASIC to create a simple picture or shape, often programming the image point by point and then printing it out on a dot matrix printer. The final work looked like a low-resolution monochrome needlepoint.

Although the programming platforms we use have changed significantly, our expectations of technology have not. If we teach programming, it is often to help prepare students for the challenges of the workplace. This goal is too far removed to be genuine or accessible to teachers in the primary grades. If we are going to say anything about the jobs a first grader will be asked to do in her life, it is only that we do not know what shape work will take in her lifetime. The goal of programming in the primary grades is not some abstract, far-off job readiness; the goal is to support learning.

Engagement, sometimes described on a continuum from boredom to inspiration, is a cocktail of influences that keeps the student's mind in the learning experience. One powerful ingredient in this mix is the joy of making something. This joy comes from creating something of your own. While building a set of shelves from a furniture store might fill us with pride, the joy of making something only comes when we give shape or voice to something yet undefined. This is why educators focus on voice and choice: we have to leave enough space in the learning experience to allow students to craft their own messages, while still guiding them enough that they feel the need to create a message.

Teaching prereaders to program is fun. Done correctly, this work is "hard fun." In class, programming is framed as – challenging play, fun that requires effort, focus, and sometimes help. Working with young students can be tricky, especially when the lessons are complex and engaging. What factors can you control when creating a digital learning experience? How long should activities be? How much programming makes sense? All of these considerations and decisions are ones that teachers have to make with their kids in mind.

No one expects teachers to be experts in programming; teachers need to be experts in kids and how they learn.

How Long Is a Lesson?

All aspects of the lesson, from the length of the task to the language and platform you use to deliver it, should be tailored to support your students. How long a class can last, at least early in the school year, will be tied directly to how challenging the work of the day is. The lesson that focuses more on group work and social skill building can be very demanding. These lessons might start as brief as twenty minutes. The goal is to switch activities before frustration builds to tears, but we shouldn't be afraid of either.

Sometimes learning can be confusing and disappointing. When students cry, it is often because they are at a total loss for what to do next. Why a student started crying is often not as important in the moment of learning as what they do next. After a brief conversation and refocusing, the student should be able to rejoin the lesson. Hard fun is hard, and sometimes it is not much fun. After focused programming and group work, the class gets to dance together using a video from GoNoodle.

Why Do We Dance?

As students get more comfortable with programming, they can write the directions to a GoNoodle video as a program. By displaying the program as they follow the video, students might choose to "read ahead" on the program to be ready for what is coming next. With or without the program displayed, group dance is a sequencing activity. Dancing is good for learning: following the directions as well as the actions on screen is cognitively demanding enough that success feels like a real accomplishment. From the reinforced skills to the awesome intrinsic reward, group dancing is a great way to end a programming lesson.

As students continue to learn about programming, they will use group dance to learn programs, and they will compose programs to lead group dances.

What Does Programming Look Like?

The Design Studio has replaced the Computer Lab, and the tables have all been pushed to the side of the room to allow more space for dancing. Students program without keyboards, and sometimes without screens. The students walk around and chat with each other. They draw the program's commands on cards and work together to place them in the right order before inputting the program. This is programming in first grade.

Sometimes students gather in groups of four to guide a bumblebee-shaped robot to the tile on the grid with the same number that is displayed on the dice. Other times they stand side by side focused together on solving an app-based challenge. When either one succeeds, four hands go up in celebration.

Programming isn't solitary or quiet. Students working in groups each have an active role. Although they regularly switch who is controlling the iPad, what they are doing is more complex than "taking turns." When programming is a group activity, the greatest challenge in designing the lesson is making sure that there are active roles for all students at all times. In some schools, technology class is limited to fifty minutes per week, so there isn't time to have students waiting during a lesson.

Although one-to-one programs are all the rage and educational institutions will often flaunt their commitment to get each student a device, rarely do we ask prereaders to go off and program on their own. One of the biggest reasons we don't ask students to work alone is that they have not yet been taught to read a tablet screen for clues for help. Without a partner to talk to, a stuck student will have to wait for a teacher to become available. Asking students to develop and practice the language and skills of collaboration is better pedagogy than one-to-one in this context. So much more can be learned when they are working and not waiting.

What Programming Languages Are Appropriate for Prereaders?

Before any person who is a computer programmer raises an objection, let us be clear. Prereaders do not use a full programming language. They use an app or system that has created visual shortcuts to common elements of programming. The visual shortcuts are designed to depict their syntax, like pieces of a puzzle. This allows very young students to have a programming-style interaction without having to read anything.

Most programming languages that are used to do work in the world are text based and require excellent literacy skills to master. With that caveat in place, there are an ever-growing array of apps, robots, and even board games that support prereaders in programming and computational thinking.

Off-line Programming

Although it is clearly designed for family play as opposed to classroom use, Robot Turtles is a board game focused on computational thinking and noncompetitive problem-solving play. Each turtle player writes programs with command cards which an adult player, as the "computer," uses to move the robot to the indicated space. The game uses no text and introduces new programming concepts in stages. One of the real strengths of the game design is that it places a conversation between the child and the adult "computer" at the center of the game play. In this interaction, the child has the power. The challenge they face is to navigate the syntax of the moves available to them.

While it would not be possible to play this game with a whole class, unless you had a 4:1 student-teacher ratio, Robot Turtles could be a choice activity or part of a programming basics learning stations rotation. The station would need an adult or an older student to lead the game, and the group would need about fifteen minutes of playtime. Teachers with the resources to do so should keep track of how often students work with the game and adjust game play to build skills as the students play the game more.

Beyond board games, there are more active off-line ways to apply programming in learning contexts for prereaders. There are many moments in the elementary classroom that can be adjusted to include code. Consider songs and dances. These can be programmed using simple notation and can be a great aid in teaching concepts of loops and subroutines. If you dance with your students, you can start coding tomorrow. Use a simple visual code to write a description of the dance the class is doing in visual markup. Look at the notation and ask students how you could make it easier to read. Be consistent when you program with your class: program left to right; once you decide on a symbol that means loop or repeat, stick with that symbol.

The great advantage of looking at programming and computational thinking expansively is that, with some work, almost any learning experience can be modified to make significant and appropriate use of programming. The goal is not to use programming for the sake of programming, but to add a layer of cognitive complexity to an existing content-area learning activity.

While off-line programming offers teachers an open door to bring any content into programming activities, programming apps offer fewer opportunities for direct content integration.

Programming Apps for Prereaders

There are several programming apps available to support prereaders learning the basics of computational thinking. While it oversimplifies the market slightly, it can be useful to think about two types of apps: leveled game-style apps and open studio apps. The leveled apps are designed to help students build their own understanding of computational thinking and programming fundamentals.

Both Kodable and The Foos ask students to navigate characters through a challenging environment using arrows and other visual commands. These leveled apps are often designed to keep a single user engaged. Teachers working with these apps have to carefully design the learning experience in order to meet social skills and communication learning goals. The work the teacher does is to build the experience around the app, not within it.

Kodable asks students to help the Fuzz Family to get the help they need. They have to navigate a world of bright blue paths, garden gnomes, and gold coins. The programming begins simply. The pieces students need to move flash, and then the place they need to drag the piece to also begins to flash. With no language written or spoken, the app can walk a new user through the basic functionality. Since the app handles basic functionality, the teacher's role is to design an experience around the app that supports more learning goals.

With Kodable, especially the early levels, there are so many great opportunities for paired programming. The first time students see the app, have them working as partners, so they can watch and then program. This helps them master the program more quickly and the pair is their own help resource.

Of course, not all students are ready to share an iPad. This sets the stage for a great lesson on collaboration and communication. Before turning the pairs of kids loose with an iPad, have a conversation about sharing. Talk about how the partner who is not currently programming can be helpful without being obnoxious.

The Foos offers many of the same learning opportunities. Using the same communication tools with each app in turn will help students understand that both programming concepts and social concepts are transferrable from one app and situation to another.

While these leveled apps are designed to support and engage the individual user, support in class implementation yields more effective learning than unsupervised use of the app. Without an adult to answer some of the questions about how the app works, students may misunderstand a concept and experience significant frustration.

Leveled apps do help build literacy skills through sequencing as well as computational thinking skills, but open studio apps, like ScratchJr, equip users with the tools needed to create an animation or a game of their own design. ScratchJr is the best, and possibly only, open studio app for prereaders, and it is free and available on Android as well as iOS. ScratchJr also supports program sharing, so a teacher can build interactive programming activities inside of the ScratchJr app and share them directly with students. This type of flexible open studio platform that supports student creation as well as sharing between students and teachers is the immediate future of programming platforms in schools.

Robots for Prereaders

The most exciting programming we can currently do with prereaders is programming robots. In the last two years, the world of educational robots has changed. We no longer have to manage the pieces and the learning curve of LEGO robotics. Through Sphero, Bee-Bots, Thymio, and Dash and Dot from Wonder Workshop, students can program robots to complete challenges long before they have enough language to use Scratch, Tynker, or the Tickle app to control robots. Perhaps the simplest of these robots is the most established in the field of education, the Bee-Bot.

The Bee-Bot features seven buttons for on bot programming. Each forward or backward command moves the bot one bot-length, 15 cm. Instructional design for the Bee-Bot is really simple. The robot can be ordered with a floor mat that is easily customized with letters, numbers, or pictures. The bumble-bee persona of the robot is whimsical, but the robot does not pretend to be a bee or run through any cute routines. This is a real benefit with younger students, as the robot only does what it is told to do.

The Bee-Bot's strength is its simplicity, but the applications are limited. For prereaders, this robot is perfect: it moves slowly and makes small mistakes. The Bee-Bot is an educational robot by design, originally created for classroom use. There are well-established resources for custom card and mat sets. It is also fairly simple to create custom content for the floor mats with Microsoft Word and a laminator. This is a great starter robot for teachers as well as students.

The other robots available present a greater instructional challenge, as they are truly connected toys we are asking to serve double-duty as instructional tools. These robots can be used very successfully as instructional tools, and the awesome part is that using them looks, sounds, and feels like play. This is an occasion of abundant engagement that teachers have to capture and channel into learning.

The Sphero robot, a motorized programmable sphere the size of a baseball, is quick, colorful, and custom designed to get kids hooked on playful learning. For prereaders, Sphero offers the Draw and Drive app available on both Android and iOS. In this app, students draw a path on the tablet screen and the robot follows that path in the classroom. Students have to aim the robot, and they discover how to control the direction, speed, and color of the robot. This simple control interface introduces students to the relationship between input and output in a much more understandable way than the remote control style interface called Drive.

When you are designing lessons with Sphero and prereaders, focus on the playful aspects of the interaction. Use the robots as an occasion to build social skills and practice problem solving. Since this robot is tablet controlled, students will be most successful in pairs. Any robot lesson begs for all the clear floor space you can manage, and fast robots, like Sphero, need larger targets on the floor. If a target is too small, a student might have the robot on the right path, but momentum will carry the robot past the target too quickly.

A fun, but by no means clean, way of getting students working together with Sphero is to make art. The Sphero robot is waterproof, a feature that isn't often useful at school. But it means we can use them with tempera paint and wash them off afterward.

The setting is pretty important for this activity. How big will the painting be? How large is your paper? How large of a wood frame can you create to corral your painting Spheros? If you don't want paint-covered robots racing all over your room, you must build a simple "box" to contain the Spheros inside the painting area. Instead of keeping the paint outside the paint area, place shallow paint dishes in the corners of the paper and drive the robots into and out of the paint.

Students place their robot in the paint, aim it, and program it by drawing on their iPad. The line they have drawn on the screen is performed by the robot, leaving a trail of paint across the paper. This activity can be adapted for older students by using a more advanced programming interface, but it is superfun for prereaders.

When Morgan's, a teacher at a school in California, first grade class painted with robots, it was a loud, messy, crazy class. The students were engaged in painting and were delighted. Painting with robots is just one fun piece of a whole system of programming activities that build fundamental literacy skills.

The adorable robot duo from Wonder Workshop makes the most of engagement and piles on the personality. Dash is a three-wheeler who can move its head independent of its wheelbase, allowing it to look around. Dot appears just to be Dash's head unit without the wheels, making Dot immobile. Dot will light up and play preprogrammed or recorded sounds.

Of the robots discussed in this text, these have the most personality and independently run several personality routines. For example, when left to charge the robot will go into sleep mode after twenty minutes. The robot announces sleep mode by yawning, looking around, and then beginning to snore. When the robot wakes, it greets you with a friendly, "Hi." These features are very cute and can be confusing to students who are learning that robots only perform their program. As we work with connected toys, we need to help students understand that the robots' "interactions" are also programs that have been installed in the robot's firmware.

Dash and Dot are programmable in a variety of apps, including Blockly and Tickle, but for prereaders, the best choice is Wonder Workshop's own Path app. Dash is programmed in the Path app as students stack icons that represent robot actions or sounds onto a line. When the play button is pressed, the robot follows the path and completes the actions described by the icons in order. This app allows students to sequence Dash's movements and personality routines into a narrative. The student's real creative skill comes in describing the story with the sequence of routines.

Lesson design with Dash and Dot places narrative at the center. Once the introduction levels of Path are completed, all of the movement, sound, and personality routines are unlocked. With access to these tools, students can create short expressive narratives that use the robot to express ideas that reach beyond programming.

Let's say the class has been reading the great children's book *Goggles* by Ezra Jack Keats. Students could program Dash and Dot to act out part of the story or extend the narrative. When we ask students to act out or reimagine a story, we do so to keep them thinking about the events and how the characters responded. When we ask them to program a robot to do this, there is a whole layer of cognitive complexity that gets added and a level of personal performance anxiety that can be removed.

When students are programming a robot to act out something, the task is not complete until they have a chance to explain what the robot is doing and why. This is how to assess a robot narrative. Students should record their robot actor and explain the actions the robot is completing. This shared video reflection is the beginning of students performing "code talks" in later grades. Even kindergarten students can make these reflective videos with support.

Thymio II is a multiple sensor robot that is the most complex robot still appropriate for prereaders. Once connected to a laptop computer, students can use a drag and drop visual programming interface to connect triggers (light, sounds, proximity) from the sensors to actions (moving forward, turning, stopping, or playing a sound). The Thymio has two motors and over twenty sensors, and it is compatible with LEGO building systems. This robot is a great tool to get kids working with prototyping and design thinking.

Lesson ideas for Thymio can be found on Sharon Marzouk's website Techykids.com. The site houses some of the lessons Sharon uses with her classes and afterschool program, as well as photos of the student's completed projects. Sharon guides her students through the design and development process, and they create something of their own that exploits some of Thymio's functionality.

The options for programming with prereaders keep growing and developing. From an educator's perspective, this is very encouraging, as the tools to bring computational thinking into the classroom become more accessible and reliable. When we ask students to work together to complete cognitively complex programming tasks, we are helping students build the skills that make reading fun and meaningful.

Chapter 5

Blockly-Based App Programming

Why Blockly?

A visual editor like Hopscotch or Tynker manages the syntax of the program through interlocking shapes. Commands that cannot work together do not fit together. This visual approach to programming is great for younger students as it simplifies the demands of syntax. Blockly is a tool for building such visual programming editors.

Students working in a visual programming editor snap commands together and select options from drop down menus instead of manually counting their own nested brackets and looking up hex codes for specific colors. Teachers, once they are familiar with the platform, can spot errors much more quickly than they could find a misplaced semicolon.

Blockly-based apps allow students to get programming fast. In a forty-five-minute class period, a student can complete multiple iterations of a functioning video game, an animation, or a model. The speed of creation is especially astonishing to anyone who has spent time working in a text-based programming syntax. The work the students are doing in Hopscotch, Tickle, and Tynker during grades two to four is preparing them to be productive in Scratch in grades four to eight.

When students work in several different apps that are based on Blockly, they are able to transfer lessons learned in one programming environment into another. The fluid use of apps also helps students practice learning how to navigate new environments. While programs written in Blockly will not usually operate outside of the programming environment they were written in, developers are making it easier for users to share their work in communities.

Hopscotch has built a great collaborative user community where users can play each other's games and then branch the program into their own project, making their own version of the game. Creative communities like this are common around programming languages, and interacting in them responsibly should be an important part of any programming curriculum.

Blockly is not a compromise; it is a developmentally appropriate scaffold for programming and computational thinking. The visual programming language relieves the user from the burden of syntax while demanding the user create. In most cases, programming apps will not simply ask students to connect a few routines in a variety of ways. Apps like Tickle, Hopscotch, and Pyonkee make as many commands available as they can support. Hopscotch was judged to be a Turing complete programming language, answering all on its own the question, "Is Blockly real programming?"

Programming in Apps

There are many tablet-based iOS and Android programming apps available, and there seem to be more every day. Check the last chapter of this text for our annotated bibliography of programming apps. Programming apps are generally categorized as leveled game-style apps or as open studio apps. The leveled apps are designed to teach the user the basic principles of programming through a gamified experience where level by level the challenges become greater.

Open studio apps aim to let the user design and build programs within the app that can often be shared with others using a community within the app or a web-based interface that connects to the app. One style of app is not superior to the other; they just do different things. When you're deciding which to use in a lesson, think about your learning goals and match the app to fit.

Leveled Programming Apps

Leveled programming apps, like Kodable, Cody's Quest by Tynker, and The Foos, use all of the mechanics of games to guide students through a process of learning a platform's tools, commands, and structures. These are introduced one at a time in the context of a challenge. Such apps can be powerful learning tools to use in whole class instruction as well as individual and choice-based learning contexts.

The apps tend to have small tutorials built into them, making them an excellent choice for teachers who don't have a great deal of programming experience. The platform can carry some of the burden of instruction. Seek out a smart platform, or at least one that can help students work their way through the challenges. Tynker has a variety of leveled experiences, and it is a recommended choice because the on-screen help is good, and the need to figure out a problem gets the kids reading.

It is unrealistic to believe that a teacher will be able to work their way through all of the levels of an app before their students use the app. Some apps do offer teachers a solution guide, often accessible behind a "teacher" button in the app or contained on their website.

Don't let the fact that the app looks like a game put you off. Students find the game-style interface very engaging, and these apps use levels, points, and rewards to keep kids engaged in learning.

Kodable

In this app, students are helping the Fuzz Family navigate through Smeeborg, a colorful world where their ship has crash-landed. The students meet a wide cast of Fuzz characters as they navigate through the levels. Kodable is designed to help students learn computer science and programming fundamentals. The app designers hope to get students engaged in computational thinking and problem solving.

As the levels progress, more complex mazes lead to opportunities to apply more advanced programming concepts. The progression takes students from simple commands (left, right, up, down) to loops and functions. Once students have mastered these levels, they advance into a different mode of gameplay that supports programming to learn about the use of variables and values in programming.

While Kodable is designed to be an engaging stand-alone game played by one child, there are some amazing supports available for teachers who wish to use Kodable as part of their technology curriculum. School support for Kodable is available through subscription. In addition to a dashboard that allows teachers to see how far students have progressed and where they have struggled, there is a customizable curriculum. The curriculum matches support lessons and printable materials with specific concepts and levels within the app. This allows teachers to script the path the students will take through the app, deciding which levels will be accessible.

An additional benefit of the school subscription is that students can access their profiles on their home tablet or through a web page. This gives access at home that still reports data to the teacher, and that the teacher can limit. If a student accesses from home, the teacher can only have some of the available lessons unlocked. This allows the teacher to use the app instructionally without students getting excited and playing all the levels at home.

The curriculum from Kodable is a great way to get students working with computational thinking and programming. The off-line activities and the class discussions present a good model of integrating technology concepts in nontechnology lessons, but does Kodable allow nontech content integration? As a leveled app, the digital side of the experience is fully constructed before the teacher has access to it. This could change when teachers have access to a level editor. For now, integration has to happen contextually. The nontech learning goals have to be handled by the environment or the design of the lesson. For instance, Kodable is a great paired programming opportunity, and in those pairs the learning objective is communication.

Asking students to problem solve together and to collaborate in programming on a single screen is a tall order—a high-challenge goal. If the activity was not fun, if it did not feel and play like a game, this goal would be too much to ask. Since we are engaged in playful learning, this goal is appropriately ambitious. The direct instruction at the head of this lesson should include modeling and discussion of communication.

Cody's Quest by Tynker

Students begin their tablet-based interaction with the Tynker app in Cody's Quest, a leveled coding tutorial featuring an adorable troll eating candy as it walks across a desktop. The app introduces elements of Blockly code one at a time. From level to level, the challenges and concepts get more advanced. The coding blocks feature text, and the concepts develop quickly in this app, which can be used in class with students as young as second grade.

Students connect Blockly commands in a programming pane to the left of the screen. The programming blocks, as well as the interface, help students become familiar with a Scratch-style programming experience. Cody operates on a simple side-view platform. As students continue through the Tynker app, they will command dragons through a multilayer platform environment and race rocket ships in a top-down game space.

Tynker has a very well-developed system of curriculum and online lessons, as well as a dashboard and student profile system. There are some levels available without a subscription, and teachers using the free version do have access to a student dashboard. This makes a great Scratch-style trainer available to any teacher with browser or tablet access to Tynker. Tynker connects many different programming experiences to one profile. The leveled app games culminate in an open studio-style game building experience. In addition to the app experience, Tynker has a full web-based open studio interface. In addition to computer science lessons, the paid subscription content includes math and STEM lessons appropriate for older students.

Cody's Quest very quickly introduces conditionals in commands, such as, "Walk forward unless you see a bottle cap, then jump over it." This requires students to think logically and gets them designing problem-solving systems, which is awesome. What else can teachers do with the Tynker app? Cody's Quest is a great tool to get kids familiar with Blockly. The third grade students in my colleague Stacy's class use the Tynker app before they begin the online Tynker tutorials. After they complete the tutorials, they use the online version of Tynker to create an animated presentation about an ecosystem. The presentation is based on research the students have done in person and online.

Stacy's class, a third grade class in a private school in California, also uses programming in Tynker as a chance to practice reflective learning. Students are asked to complete a "code talk," taking a screenshot of the game and narrating an explanation of how they solved the challenge. Once they have completed this short video, they e-mail it to the private class blog, and it is displayed on-screen at the front of the room.

The Foos

The Foos is a platform-style game in which each group of levels places the student in command of a different character with different special abilities. Students use visual programming commands, arrows for direction, and icons for special abilities and functions. The app is appropriate for prereaders and introduces new concepts and commands gradually, allowing users ample playtime to get comfortable with the commands. The levels are grouped, and each group has a free play level which allows users to interact with characters with no specific goal in mind. This is not an open studio interaction, but a free play one. The students cannot control the setting or add objects or characters beyond a limited range of choices.

The Foos does not currently offer a dashboard, but codeSpark, makers of The Foos, do offer online curriculum and support. There is also a solution guide that includes some great programming Easter eggs, like how to get "The Glitch" to throw hotdogs. Currently in development, "Foos Studio" will allow users to create their own levels to extend play and engagement.

As with other leveled apps, teachers can connect this app to learning through narrated video reflection or social skills development. The game changer will be when the level editor is available. Once students can design their own levels, they could create a level of The Foos that represented a natural system like the geosphere, or a new level could retell a story the class had read together. The act of creating a game level becomes an act of author-ship focused on metaphorical thinking. Once we can use programming to get students engaged in this level of cognitive complexity around subject area content, we have seriously boosted the intellectual attention and engagement which students bring to the interaction.

The Pace of Learning in Leveled Apps

As a teacher, you will notice that the apps self-differentiate. Students work quickly through the levels they "get" and have to spend more time on others.

Pairing students appropriately for paired programming is something that must be done with the goal in mind. Are the pairs selected for quiet problem solving going to be the same pairs selected if the goal is conflict resolution? Even though the leveled apps can be fairly self-contained, using them in the classroom is not a simple matter of handing out iPads. There are a few tricks and structures that can help support student learning and success.

Tips for Teaching Code with Leveled Apps

1. Don't undercut the tutorials. Many of the apps have a good library of built-in tutorials. Ask your students to engage the tutorials and "read the screen," or look for tips and solutions in the app. This is part of the problem-solving process. You are teaching them to find and discover the answer. We want students to look for the answer themselves. If we create instruction that replicates the tutorial information, we are teaching students to look to someone else for the answer, undercutting both the instructional nature of the leveled app and robbing them of a chance to develop their critical reading skills.

    Yes, problem solving in an app that actually contains the answers they need is a type of critical reading. As a teacher, you have to avoid reinforcing the idea that the teacher will have all the answers. You have to replace this expectation with the experience that the work environment will have the answers they are looking for.

2. Focus on communication and problem solving. Since the app is going to do the heavy lifting of teaching the programming concepts, this frees you up to teach the important things, like how to ask another student for help, or how to notice when someone needs some help and how to offer it, or how to politely refuse help when you want to work through a problem on your own.

3. Hang back and watch body language. Observation can yield a great deal of data. A general guide is this: fist pumps = good, face in hands = bad. If you want your students to problem solve and ask each other for help, you have to make yourself a little less available. You have to support their struggling by not allowing them to shortcut past problem solving. If you want to teach resilience, you have to put up some roadblocks to them relying on you. Don't cash in on the good feeling you get when you offer short-term help; invest in long-term problem solving.

4. Build in some reflection. One of the greatest challenges to teaching with a self-contained leveled app is that it can be hard to tell how the students are doing other than what you observe. Ask your students to take screenshots as they work when they are stuck, or when they solve a particularly challenging level. At the end of the class, give them five to eight minutes to use SonicPics or another photo narration app to create a narrated slide

show or ebook of their work, using the screenshots and describing their successes and challenges.

Once they have these recorded, have them share the short recordings to the class blog, or use a cloud computing service like Google Drive to share them directly with you. This gives you a much better insight into how they are meeting the challenge and gets them to think about the learning they have done. This type of reflective thinking is often the difference between playing and learning, so even when your time with the kids is limited, make time for reflective thinking.

Open Studio Apps

Open studio programming apps, like ScratchJr, Tickle, the create side of Tynker, and Hopscotch, require a very different support strategy in the primary grades. An open studio app does not have levels, goals, points, stars, or any built-in motivational supports. Teachers using an open studio app need to create a complete educational experience, using strategies of sharing and communication to keep students engaged and motivated.

Any teacher who has taught writing will be familiar with one of the greatest challenges in an open studio app, the challenge of the blank white page. When students open Hopscotch or ScratchJr, they can do anything. This infinite potential can be a huge problem.

A common question from students is, "What do I do?" While this is a problem for kids working independently, it is an opportunity for teachers. The open design leaves space for meaningful connection to the content being studied in class. It can be challenging to make content-area learning connections in a leveled app because it is a closed system; each level was written long before the app was placed in front of a student. Open studio apps become easier to use and more meaningful when you make classroom learning, not the programming itself, the focus of the activity.

ScratchJr

Developed specifically for use by prereaders, ScratchJr is a tablet version of the popular programming language Scratch. This open studio app facilitates creative play by making it easy for users to design narrative scenes and create simple interactive programs. Although the program loads with the familiar Scratch the Cat on the stage, users can add any character they want, either from the impressive in-app library of characters or by drawing their own characters in the app. There is even the option to use the camera on the tablet to import a character, so students can place themselves in the program they have designed.

Instead of focusing on how to use the app to teach computer science concepts, the focus with ScratchJr was on how to create an app that allowed kids to create awesome stuff. Since this is the case, there are no built-in tutorials available in the app. There are great resources available online, including eight tutorial activities that can be downloaded as PDFs. Unlike other apps, the team behind ScratchJr is not trying to generate any revenue. The good news is that this means all of the functionality is yours for free; the bad news is that you cannot just pay for extra help or content. Like many of the resources mentioned in this book, some of the best support for this tool is available in online communities of teachers using this app.

Without a doubt this is the most powerful programming platform available for prereaders today. Given the ability to create complex narratives, dialogues, record custom sound, and support multiple custom backgrounds, the instructional potential of this app is staggering. Without much direct instruction in this app students can begin to connect directly to content from class. The first project by Morgan's first graders, a class at a private school in California, using ScratchJr is to create a moving model of the coral reef. The programming is simple: basic motion commands plus a loop command. Students can describe the inhabitants of the reef and how they interact.

Currently only supported on iOS, ScratchJr does allow users to send program files to each other. Instructionally, this means that teachers can build a partial program and send it to students. This is amazing, because it allows teachers to design an "in app" learning experience. The Kindergarten students first used this feature to spell sight words. The teacher set up a file with scrambled student names and students had to use programming to unscramble them. As programming platforms become more full-featured, the ability to share full or partial programs will become more commonplace.

Hopscotch, Scratch, and the web version of Tynker use online communities to share projects, while Tickle and ScratchJr share files directly between devices or e-mail addresses. These projects are shared in a way that allows others to use and rewrite the programs. This is sometimes called branching and other times called remixing. Teachers can use these sharing features to share a partial program with students. This can get a whole class started, or just make sure the class is using a common media library. In addition, teachers can give extra help to students by giving them scaffolded versions of the program to clarify the task or provide a concrete example.

Hopscotch

Hopscotch is sometimes referred to as Scratch for iPads, which isn't completely fair, but is still correct on many points. Hopscotch is a Blockly-based open studio app that allows students to build and share interactive stories, art, and games. From recursive geometric drawings to building a working version of Flappy Bird, Hopscotch is a powerful programming language and a very accessible interface for students who are reading at the second to third grade level. There is no code visible on the main stage of the app, but once a sprite is selected the screen displays the programming window for that character.

Hopscotch is a Turing complete programming language, which means that it can be used to meet many different ends. From drawing in second grade to scientific modeling in fifth, Hopscotch is a powerful open studio app that allows students to successfully create programs quickly. For a great read on teaching with open studio apps, download Wes Fryer's Hopscotch ebook. Dr. Fryer walks the reader through the design of challenge-based lessons to keep kids engaged and focused while learning Hopscotch. Challenges that focus on one or two skills can make the app less overwhelming.

Hopscotch is focused on individual users and has few tools available to educators. One tool is the curriculum. Hopscotch offers parents and teachers a simple set of lesson plans to help kids use Hopscotch and understand what they are doing. The other tool Hopscotch has is the community. Although this is not designed exclusively for educators, savvy teachers can share the assignment project to the community and then have students navigate to it and branch, or remix, the project.

In this model, the project is analogous to a handout; when the students remix the project, they make a copy of the handout. With luck and planning, the activities the students engage in will be so awesome that this handout analogy will seem ridiculous, but it is meant to simply illustrate how the Hopscotch community can be used to distribute instructional materials.

Instructionally, Hopscotch is a powerhouse. Since it acts much like Scratch, all of the instructional opportunities for programming in education developed over the last twenty-five years are on the menu, so to speak. Hopscotch turns a tablet computer into a digital spirograph, allowing teachers to use the geometry lessons perfected using Turtle Art and other versions of LOGO.

Modern geometry instruction that does not use Hopscotch to teach regular polygons is missing the boat. The concept of repeated angle and side measures is perfectly highlighted when students program the polygon using a repeat function. When they asked how big the angles would be on an eight-sided shape, second graders learned order of operations while asking Siri to divide 360 by the number of sides in a polygon, so they would know the angle measure.

Acknowledging Hopscotch's deep resources for math instruction, we must also mention the impact of using Hopscotch for modeling. As students study science, they often learn about processes or systems. Programming allows them to simulate or model these processes or systems. When students program a model of a system, they have to be able to describe the behavior of each component of the system as well as any interrelationships. This is exactly the type of work middle schoolers can do in Scratch.

Asking fourth and fifth grade students to program a model requires them to think procedurally and also describe the roles and actions of parts of a system in detail. In a world asking more and more for conceptual understanding of problems, not merely solutions, Hopscotch is a platform that helps students focus on designing a program and not simply solving a problem.

Tickle

The Tickle app brings the power of Blockly coding to the Internet of things and the world of connected toys. Connecting to robots like Sphero, Ollie, and Dash and Dot, Tickle empowers students to take their programming skills off the screen and into the real world. The commands available in the menu change to fit the robot, light, drone, or sprite you are programming. The commands are placed into a programming window in a style users of Scratch and Hopscotch will recognize. In addition to having all the functionality a Scratch user would expect, Tickle allows users to collect data from the robots' sensors and use it to trigger actions in other connected devices. A savvy student could program a drone to lift off when the Sphero robot crashes.

There are currently many great robot lessons taught every day using Sphero and Tickle or Dash and Dot and Tickle. Although the Tickle website is not thick with lesson resources, its Facebook page and Twitter profile are. Tickle is a young app working hard to expand functionality, and teachers everywhere are using it to connect robots to a continuum of Blockly-based coding. The real power of this programming is not in a particular app, but in the fact that students can move from one app to another without a long relearning period.

Instructionally, Tickle is a great way to get students to look again at aspects of programming they had only viewed in two dimensions. Drawing a square in Hopscotch and making a robot drive a square in Tickle are related but slightly different programs. Doing both will help a student understand squares a bit better than just having the student do one or the other.

It is possible to share programs directly using Tickle, so teachers can differentiate and scaffold lessons using Tickle effectively. Students can share programs with each other as they work, a feature that teachers should use to help students understand how to give credit responsibly and work in a creative community. The Tickle app is a great tool to keep the use of robots in the classroom focused on instruction and programming instead of remote control racing, which often happens when using the apps that ship with the robots.

Tynker Game Builder

The Tynker app is three parts leveled app and one part open studio game builder. Once the users have completed the levels in-app, they are well prepared to design their own video games in the game design side of the app. Even there, the experience is not the same as the blank canvas approach of ScratchJr or Hopscotch. Tynker game builder has commands and actions packaged into groups to help students get started quickly. Without packaged movements, command like "walk" would require users to program the location of the upper and lower legs, and the upper and lower arms.

Tynker has deep resources on its website and in the online learning community. As mentioned above in the leveled apps section, Tynker is a great solution for schools looking for a single platform for home and school, tablet, and web browser. There is an online curriculum as well as downloadable lessons, and a large community of teachers uses Tynker to support computer science as well as subject area learning.

Subscribing to Tynker is like signing up for a well-supported version of Scratch, and it might be a great solution for a school system that wants more teachers and kids programming but does not have the internal resources to support and train teachers.

The web version of Tynker has a wider range of learning opportunities, but what has been said of other game design platforms holds true here. When we ask students to create a game or interactive program about something we are learning in class, we are asking students to think metaphorically and create an abstract representation of something we have learned. Asking students to create a game that depicts one aspect of history might turn up a timeless gem like "Oregon Trail." No matter what the students build in the game designer, no matter how well it works, assessment comes from listening to them explain their game and what it means.

Pyonkee

Hopscotch may have been referred to as Scratch for the iPad, but Pyonkee looks exactly like the Scratch user interface compacted to fit the iPad and with a slightly different cast of characters. It is based on Scratch's open source code. Users can program by dragging commands from a programming field on the left of the screen, exactly as they do in the online and resident versions of Scratch. The app works fairly well considering that they have managed to accomplish what the Scratch team has not been willing to creates a version of Scratch that does not use Flash. The app is socially challenged at times, and it is not always easy to use the scroll bars attached to the programming windows.

Pyonkee version 1.9 is able to import existing Scratch projects via AirDrop. This powerful upgrade should make it much easier to use Pyonkee on the iPad instructionally. As we noted with Tickle and ScratchJr, the ability to save and share projects makes it much easier for teachers to build assignments and share them with students. Since the app is based directly on Scratch, many of the necessary support pieces have already been written for Scratch and may apply directly to Pyonkee.

With all of the power of Scratch and portable files, Pyonkee should be the most powerful tablet-based programming app out there. The app is very young, having just celebrated the one-year anniversary of its release. As the platform improves, more students and teachers will exploit the recently added cross functionality with Scratch.

Leveled apps introduce one tool at a time, but when students enter an open studio app, they have the full menu available to them right away. Choice can be hard, especially when there is no clear goal. Open studio apps are powerful partners for learning, but they come with some built-in challenges, so here are some great practices to support engagement and success using open studio apps in the classroom.

Tips for Teaching with Open Studio Apps

1. Balance direction and discovery. When students figure out something for themselves, they own that knowledge. They experience a reward greater than any stars or points can trigger. The role of the teacher is to get them to the point where they are ready to discover something.

   In an open studio app, this means teaching one or two tools at a time and setting a challenge focused on those tools. Directions for open studio app work in the classroom have to be much more detailed than directions for leveled app work because there is very little learning support in the open studio app. Students need to be introduced to tools through a video or live demonstration, and this should be supported by screenshots of significant pieces of base code or multiple starter programs.

   Teachers can support students by sending them partial programs and making code resources available in class. Sample code projected to the front of the room can be a powerful model. Further differentiation can be achieved by having more code available on extra devices. If a student is struggling, the teacher can work next to the student, showing them some important pieces of code to help them get past their roadblock.

   Try to limit the number of blocks introduced in any class to two or three, and ask students to do something meaningful with those blocks. Choice is important, but if students are spending too much time with other commands or functions, the challenge can help them get back on track.

2. Connect the challenge to content. Open studio apps are great for connecting to content. If the lesson is about loops, and students have been learning about coral reef life, have them create an animation where fish and reef animals swim back and forth. A programming lesson focused on teaching the mechanics of message can support creating a dialogue about anything the students have been studying in class.

   Once students are asked to apply class content in a programming lesson, be prepared to add spelling and word wall help as they start writing more sentences into their programs. Students creating conversations between characters become really engaged in applying class content. The programming challenge becomes fun and transparent as students become invested in the challenge of creating something new with their knowledge.

3. Know the platform. The teacher needs to understand how open studio apps, like ScratchJr, Tickle App, or Hopscotch, work. There are good tutorials available for each, and preparing to teach with one of these requires spending time with the tutorials. Have fun with it and create silly projects. The key to knowing how to do something is to do it many times, often poorly.

   With open studio apps, a teacher needs to make many projects in order to try out as many of the tools as possible. The more the teacher in the room knows, the greater an asset they become. Before you teach your students how to make a dialogue in ScratchJr, create your own six-minute production. It will most likely take about an hour of your time, but afterwards, you'll really know how dialogue triggers work. The time you invest in learning the platform will pay off when you share your creation with your students.

   You don't have to be a programmer, but a basic knowledge of the platform and access to resources is important with an open studio app.

4. Design a digital learning experience. If the app allows you to do so, prep for a lesson by designing a code project populated with activities. In the learning through code chapters, you will read some detailed examples of this.

   In general, imagine that instead of creating a packet of work for a student to do with a photocopier, the work was created inside the tablet computer. Instead of depending on a software company to design meaningful learning activities, teachers can now build these activities themselves inside open studio programming apps like Hopscotch and ScratchJr.

   When teachers take the time to create a programming activity that asks students to unscramble their classmates' names, it means more than random names pulled from a book. Tablet computers are mobile and flexible, and the lessons we deliver with them should reflect that.

5. Use Guided Access to protect your learning focus. We cannot restrict our device without restricting the students, and Internet filters can be really annoying. That being said, try using Guided Access on the iPad. Filed under Accessibility Controls and Education in the Settings menu, Guided Access allows the teacher to turn off parts of the screen and disable the home and power buttons.

When teaching kindergarten students with iPads, Guided Access can help them stay in the app. By disabling the home button and turning off key parts of the screen, teachers can make it much easier for students to stay in the app.

The Role of Programming Apps in Learning

Programming apps appropriate for K-2 grade students use very little text and usually restrict the number of possible functions and the complexity of the language. Platforms like ScratchJr, The Foos, and Kodable are designed to be very successful and motivating experiences.

Part of the goal with programming at a young age is to have students develop the schema that programming is something they can do and something they can learn. As teachers, this means we have to model that programming is something we can learn and something we can do. When we take the time to connect programming to our lessons and make it part of formative assessment, students see how to use programming as a tool for communication.

When your students are building skills, use leveled apps. Kodable and The Foos should get class time early in the year with kindergarten and first grade students. Let leveled apps teach them about conditionals, loops, and functions. As you move to open studio apps, talk about the tools with your students and allow them to make connections to other platforms.

As a teacher, you don't have to be a programming expert, but you should know each platform well enough to help the students transfer understanding from one app to the other.

Chapter 6

Scratch and Other Web-Based Programming Platforms

If you have made it this far in the book and you do not yet have your own Scratch account, take a moment now and go to Scratch.org and set up one for yourself. Scratch is the most popular, best supported, and most well developed of the visual programming languages available, and it is free and open to all to use.

WHAT IS SCRATCH?

Scratch is a visual block-based programming language that facilitates creation. Programmers of almost any age can create animations, movies, and games using the block-based visual syntax. Version 1.0 of Scratch was released in 2007. This Turing complete language has over ten million users in its worldwide community. Currently, there is a desktop version of Scratch (Scratch 2.0) available for download, and a web version (Scratch 1.4) available for use online. Most Scratch projects can be completed using the web-based Scratch, but there are more advanced projects that connect to hardware, like LEGO WeDo and Hummingbird Robotics, which require a desktop version of Scratch with some custom extension libraries installed.

Is It Real Programming?

In a very real way, the answer to the question is yes. Scratch is a real programming language. It does all of the things a programming language needs to do. Scratch is a great tool in education because the visual syntax lowers the difficulty of learning. Once students are learning in Scratch, they can do some seriously complex things, within limits.

49

Scratch is a great language for learning programming concepts that can be transferred to other platforms. The syntax of a program will not transfer from a Scratch program to a Java Applet, but the programming fundamentals do. The perceived weakness of Scratch, that it won't make stand-alone apps or games, is actually the pedagogical strength of the platform. The focus is on process, not on the product. Even in the public project galleries, the focus is on branching and remixing. Students might play or watch another's program, but before long they are rewriting it to suit their own ideas.

Scratch gets users programming fast and focused on concepts, not colons. In an educational setting, this free programming language can be a powerful instructional tool. Scratch can be used to create models, simulations, animations, and interactive games. The web version has an embed feature that makes it simple for teachers and students to include Scratch projects on class blogs and school web pages.

The most capable version of Scratch is 2.0, a program that runs locally on a PC or Mac computer. The more widely accessible, web-based version of Scratch is version 1.4. This web version of Scratch is an online community in addition to a programming platform. Some schools are hesitant to use Scratch online, since students need an account of their own. The simplest solution is to ask parents for their permission and have the students enter their parent's e-mail during sign-up. If there are students who do not have parental permission, they can use the resident version of Scratch, and, if needed, load starter programs directly into Scratch instead of using the online community.

Chromebooks will run the web version of Scratch, making it a perfect platform for middle school classes with available Chromebooks. There are tablet-based programs that are clearly inspired by Scratch, like Pyonkee and Hopscotch, but there is not yet a functional Scratch app.

Considering the continuum of programming from kindergarten through fifth grade, the starting point is off-line programming and the end point is Scratch. A middle school student equipped with Scratch literacy is ready to build models and simulations, ready to explain how a program works, and ready to learn another programming language when the need arises.

WHO CAN USE SCRATCH?

There are first grade teachers working successfully in Scratch to get students programming. The teachers design appropriate challenges and directly teach about the tools needed for each challenge. Scratch does require reading. The better the students read, the easier it will be for them to use Scratch. Students who are not yet strong readers can build literacy skills while using Scratch, especially if the learning experience is designed to support literacy skill acquisition.

In many ways, the time spent programming in Scratch builds literacy and logic skills. It's a great way to support literacy, problem solving, and growth mindset. What has not been mentioned enough is that Scratch is *fun*. It is a high-engagement environment. Teachers can leverage the engaging environment to meet some demanding pedagogical goals, from social skills to chemistry.

Scratch is the programming language all primary level teachers should learn. Understanding Scratch and experiencing programming are prerequisites to teaching with Scratch. The teacher does not have to know everything about the language, but the level of exposure and understanding needs to be much greater than some of the app-based leveled programming interfaces. Once Scratch is understood, many of the other apps and languages will be easy to work with. Almost all of these platforms share design and functionality with Scratch.

Scratch is an open-studio programming environment, so it does not carry the burden of instruction or have built-in tutorial levels. The best way to get students ready to use Scratch is to have them work in a variety of block-based programming applications. When they first come to Scratch, a foundational understanding of Blockly-based programming will get students programming quickly, although they will still need to look up or figure out a few things.

There are many books and web pages to learn Scratch. A good video course can be found at learnscratch.org. Teachers working through the lessons will discover how they best learn about programming and will, hopefully, be a better teacher for that learning experience. If you are working with students who have done no programming before, it may be necessary to work with the students and guide them through some Scratch tutorials.

SCRATCH IN THE CLASSROOM

There is not a specific education version of Scratch, because Scratch was originally built as a learning tool. There are several features of the online version of Scratch that make it easy to use in an instructional capacity. Scratch.org features an organized community that teachers and students can use together. The community allows users to create their own studio and invite other users to join. This allows a teacher to set up a class studio and invite all of the students to join the studio. Once the students are in the studio, they can easily find each other's programs, leave comments, and play or remix the programs.

Remix Edu

When students remix a program in Scratch, they get their own copy of the program to modify, and, through developing the full program, they make it their own. The remix function is especially useful in the classroom, as it allows the teacher to upload a program and invite the students to remix. In this case, the teacher would not upload a complete program, but a program containing all of the work materials for the day.

If you are asking students to create a craft project, you might supply them with glue and paper. When we ask students to program about something we are learning, the remix function in Scratch makes it easy to set up a program that has the pieces they will need. If we are programming about the rainforest, the starter program might have some specific animals loaded in as characters and perhaps a custom background or two.

The remix ability is a very important feature, because it facilitates digital lesson creation as well as advanced support and differentiation for students with learning challenges. Just as the teacher can create one program and invite students to remix the provided assets, teachers can create pieces of scaffolding and share them with students using the class studio community. This means that students with learning challenges can get discrete help, and these help files can be easily available to anyone in the class, even parents and tutors should the need arise. Often students need a piece of sample code or a minimally functional program to look at in order to get past their own hurdles.

The Power of Sharing

One of the greatest features of Scratch is the shareable nature of all the published projects. Once users have published a project, it is visible in their studio, and they can easily share it to the class studio, giving access to the program to any user in Scratch. The impressive part comes when the students share the program via direct link or embed with people who are outside of the Scratch community. This means that a teacher could embed a student project on the class blog, or the school could share direct links on the school Facebook community.

Programming becomes a much more powerful text when it is shared. Just as we urge teachers to have students write for a genuine audience, we need to ask students to program for a real audience, and then do the work needed to find the program that audience. When students see that others are viewing and using their program, it changes the nature of the work. Programming stops being about one user getting a machine to do something, and it begins to focus on one user and a machine creating a text to be interacted with by another user on another machine.

Sharing programs creates opportunities to have students self-assess and reflect on the process, while giving their audience complete access to the project they made. When we ask students to write, the audience is often limited, unless we get them blogging and then share that writing to a broader community, for them. With Scratch programs, the texts are easier for others to consume, and they look more interesting than writing.

When student programs are shared, other users ask questions. Sometimes they want to know how to do a specific thing or where to find an asset. This is genuine communication stemming from a shared program. When students see this, they know the work is being viewed and played. This connection to the real world can change the way students approach the work in the classroom.

The Problem with Sharing

When students share their work, it can transform the experience profoundly. The challenge for teachers and schools is how to manage that sharing in a way that is safe and protect student privacy. Scratch.org users can comment on published projects by any user, and it is not difficult for users to communicate with each other. This is a feature for creating a collaborative community, but a liability in an educational setting. In some schools, they just install Scratch locally on machines, not allowing students to access Scratch.org specifically because of concerns about student profiles. Other schools only allow online Scratch for grades six and up, requesting parental consent.

Anytime we work with students in an online community, it is important that we discuss it with parents beforehand and give them access to that community. Parents need to understand the public nature of communities like those on Scratch.org. They also need to understand the benefit you are looking to realize. If you want to use Scratch on Chromebooks, you will need the online version. In that case you have to sell the parents on the power of the community and invite them in. Have parents make accounts and add them to the studio. Even if all the parents do not take you up on the invitation, you will be building an environment of inclusion and transparency.

What Can Students Learn in Scratch?

Scratch in two words is fast and flexible. The visual syntax and wealth of commands and functionality make it possible for students to do good work quickly. Although programming can be slow as you learn the platform, once users understand how to copy and paste code, work can speed up greatly. If you want to be truly impressed, open a browser window to Scratch.org and look through the gallery. Notice the wide variety of programs. Some are complex and amazing and others were obviously made by new users.

The evidence in the gallery suggests that almost anything can be made with Scratch, but there are a few Scratch genres that fit particularly well into classroom learning:

- Narrative projects
- Presentations
- Animated models
- Problem solvers/calculators
- Meaningful games

In addition to Scratch providing a great tool for students to show what they understand, introducing programming as a mode of learning and understanding can help teachers shift the focus of a lesson to a more conceptual level. Each of these project genres fits well into established assignments and expectations, while offering an invitation to transform lessons and make learning more meaningful through direct application of knowledge.

Narrative Projects

If you are new to programming, the idea of a narrative project might seem surprising, but narrative and programming work very well together. In a story, there is a clear sequence of events, just as there is in programming. Scratch is very well suited to empower users to animate a short dialogue and bring it to life. This is a great piece for content integration, as you can have students create a dialogue about anything the class is currently learning. The second step is that students have to create or select the actors and background for the dialogue. Then the user has to program in each piece of the dialogue and set up the actual mechanics of the dialogue. In the end, they have a short narrative of their own making that can be embedded on a web page or e-mailed home to share.

Presentations

If everyone keeps complaining about bad PowerPoint presentations, will we eventually stop using them in schools? Only if we adopt a better method, and Scratch might be it. With the ability to import custom backdrops, Scratch empowers students to leave boring presentations behind and use it to build an interactive presentation. PowerPoint becomes less problematic if you just use it as a background creator and allow Scratch to drive the presentation.

Students can build slides in PowerPoint, export them as pictures, and use them as the background in a Scratch program. Once the slides are in Scratch, students can attach timings to the slide, or program an on-screen button that will advance to the next slide. Since the presentation is created inside of

Scratch, it is easy to add animated narrative elements, models, and interactive pieces.

Moving from PowerPoint into Scratch shifts the role of the audience from passive to active, and it shifts the emphasis for the presenter from delivering a good live performance to creating a meaningful interactive experience. This gets students thinking about the role of the audience and makes it easier for students to interact with every presentation, all without shutting down class for two days to listen to speeches. If you are teaching in a programming-enabled classroom, instead of asking for a speech on the biography of a past president, ask for an interactive presentation. Once the students are competent in Scratch, encourage them to use video and sound if it is available.

Replacing the one-to-many presentation with the design of a one-to-one interactive experience is simply updating our models. When we do talk about presentations, we rarely say speeches. The TED talks we like are powerful because they are speeches. The slide deck is mostly wordless images or graphics, while the orator is front and center. So instead of asking students to build a bad PowerPoint, have them create an interactive tutorial about a past president. If the learning goal of giving a presentation is to demonstrate understanding of the researched topic, the interactive presentation could do a better job than a conventional speech.

Animated Models

When fifth grade students are studying earth systems, and they are trying to understand the geosphere from a textbook graphic, it is difficult to visualize what is really happening between the mantle and the crust of the earth. With Scratch, we can ask students to build animated models of systems and processes. It could be something as simple as photosynthesis or as complex as the behavior of molecules in different states of matter. When we want students to understand how things relate to one another, programming with Scratch can help illustrate the relationship more clearly than a static two-dimensional creation.

Problem Solvers/Calculators

One of the greatest challenges in math instruction is getting students to focus on conceptual understanding of the math illustrated by a problem. This is largely because teachers keep placing students in the role of problem solvers. If instead we ask students to design a program that solves a certain type of problem and give them five "test case" problems, the focus shifts to how the math works and how to depict that in programming.

When students write an interactive calculator program, they have to understand which operations are done in what order. They also have to be able to present the solution to the problem in the proper context. Working at this level with math gives students a context to talk about math conceptually because they are working with it conceptually. We can't give students practical math and expect conceptual results.

Meaningful Games

If your grade school technology education happened after 1983, there is a really good chance it included the game Oregon Trail. Oregon Trail might be called a settler simulator. Using landmarks (forts and rivers) and conditions (dysentery, cholera) lifted straight from history, the game helped students understand some of the deadly challenges in the trip West. Oregon Trail can serve as a template for the type of game our students can create in Scratch. In fact, using Scratch students can create a much better looking game than Oregon Trail's old school green typeset graphics.

Scratch Resources

With a truly giant user community, Scratch has many resources out there, with the best ones connected to the Scratch wiki page. Even if you teach younger students, a knowledge of Scratch can help you see how the apps and robots we use in the younger grades lead up to using Scratch in fourth grade and beyond.

OTHER WEB-BASED PLATFORMS

Web-based programming is really the only choice for classrooms using Chromebooks or desktop computers that cannot have programs installed upon them. Scratch is not the only option for in-browser programming, but it does command a large share of the attention. Scratch is an open studio app, as are some of the other in-browser programming options, but leveled apps and programming tutorial programs are much more common.

Kodable

A favorite with prereaders on the iPad, Kodable also has a web version that can be played on a Chromebook. The game play is identical to the tablet app. Players have to put commands in sequential order to help the Fuzz navigate through the levels and return to its home planet. Kodable is a leveled, game-style programming interface in which users solve puzzles. Screen by screen, more advanced tools are introduced. The web version does work with the Kodable school accounts, and students can use Kodable on the web to access the same profile they use on tablets during the school day.

CodeMonkey

CodeMonkey is a web-based leveled app focused on getting young students to work with the text-based code. In a marketplace dominated by visual programming, CodeMonkey puts students in front of a simple text code. In the challenges, the player is helping a monkey navigate a simple maze. If the user wants the monkey to move fifteen steps forward, she types, "step 15." If the monkey needs to turn right, the user types, "turn right."

Even though it is text-based programming, CodeMonkey is designed to support students who may struggle with typing. Each of the common commands—"Step," "Turn," "Left," and "Right"—has a push button on-screen that enters the command into the program when the button is pressed. Instead of using an on-screen grid like ScratchJr, CodeMonkey has a ruler built into the interface; once you click on the ruler, it will measure the distance between the next two points clicked. So to measure the distance between the monkey and the banana, the user clicks the ruler, then the monkey, and finally the banana. The ruler displays the distance as twenty, so the user types, "step 20."

CodeMonkey supports class management and at-home play connected to the class profile. The teacher dashboard empowers the teacher to control which levels the students can access. Subscribing users can use the challenge builder to create their own levels. This feature moves CodeMonkey from a leveled app experience to an open studio-style interaction.

CodeCombat

CodeCombat is a leveled adventure game-style programming platform. As their knight, wizard, or thief navigates the game, players type commands using Python or Javascript and learn about the syntax of those languages. This web-based programming environment is a fun and engaging way to get kids feeling good about syntax and text-based coding.

The adventure game is pretty low-key, but there are battles and losses and death. The leveled platform does not create significant opportunities for lesson design. CodeCombat is a great option for programming choice time. For some students looking to get into text-based coding, it lowers the entry point and provides the motivation they need to get into the syntax of Javascript.

Tynker

Tynker is an all-in-one web-based programming platform with integrated instructional components. The functionality in the web version of Tynker is very similar to Scratch, the difference being in the user support available. Tynker provides on-screen help as well as a full curriculum of tutorials.

Even in the free version of Tynker, teachers can create accounts for students and assign tutorials. The students can share their work in a class showcase. As students work through the tutorials, instructions appear on-screen. This is programming supporting reading, because students have to read the information on the screen and figure out what they are to do next.

After students have completed a few of the tutorial courses, they are ready to create their own animated presentation. Third graders were challenged by the tutorials and ultimately successful in creating their animated projects. The students who did the best in these lessons were the ones who were not technology confident. The students who had prior experience in Scratch struggled with the tutorials because they did not read the directions. The tutorials in Tynker are structured to restrict the tools available until the instructions call on that tool. The tech-savvy students found this frustrating and expressed their feelings.

The strength of the platform is apparent in the tutorials and the students' ability to access their work from any web browser, even connecting with their profile in the app. The ecosystem of instruction, connectivity, and sharing that Tynker offers is exactly the support teachers and students need to use programming instructionally.

Chapter 7

Learning with Robots

Lesson Design in Three Dimensions

The idea of teaching young children by playing with robots seems both amazing and laughable. If it's funny or strange, that's only because it is difficult to imagine learning with a robot. Spoiler alert: it will not involve C3PO lecturing your students.

Learning with robots through programming and group work is a very kinesthetic form of learning. Understanding the roles a robot can play will help you design engaging and meaningful lessons. The role a robot can play in a lesson does depend on what a robot can do. While this text refers to several different robots, these are just a few of the ever-expanding selection of educational robots. For the most current and updated information about these robots, be sure to check BeyondtheHourofCode.com.

ROBOT AS POINTER

From the Desktop to Floor

Great news! You have lessons written that are almost robot ready. The most important element in a robot lesson is to make the location of the robot meaningful. A matching activity designed for desktop work can be adapted quickly to a robot activity. Many lessons take only two steps to convert from desktop to robot lesson:

1. Enlarge the images used in the desktop activity and place them on the floor.
2. Have students working in groups program a robot to move from the image to its match.

59

With this simple idea, you can place answers to math problems on the floor and have students navigate to the right answer once they have solved the problem. Students could also roll dice and navigate to the correct answer. This model of using the robot as a pointer to indicate the correct answer was the seed of a lesson in my colleague Tali's kindergarten class. The robot used in this lesson was a Bee-Bot, a very simple robot that looks like a bumblebee and has a small wheelbase. It is programmed by pressing directional buttons on top of the robot. Every time the Bee-Bot moves, it moves 15 cm. The Bee-Bot runs on a grid of 15 sq. cm.

The objectives of this lesson:

1. Students will develop math skills (differentiated by skill).
2. Students will develop communication skills through group collaboration.

Planning this lesson requires knowledge of the students and their math abilities, but with this knowledge you can do some very meaningful differentiation. Tali had six robots to work with, so she divided her twenty-four students into six groups. She did not create groups of equal numbers. Instead, she created groups of similar math ability. With ability groups, she was able to customize the challenge level of the work to fit the students' needs. Tali ensured engagement through differentiation.

The Groups

The core of this lesson is students do the math at hand and navigate the robot to the correct answer. Tali gave each group appropriate math to do and customized the robot's grid with the answers needed.

The first group had two dice, and they were using a grid numbered 124. Even though they only used 112, the twenty-four square grid allows teachers to add a die if the students master the first activity. Of the next three groups, two used three dice and one used four dice. Each of these groups used a twenty-four square grid numbered 124. For this activity, the numbers were placed sequentially on the grid to reinforce number sequence. Placing the numbers randomly on the grid is not needed nor is it beneficial.

The fifth group was working from a problem sheet of two digit addition problems. All of the problems on the sheet had multiples of five as a solution. The answer grid was filled with multiples of five, including the solutions to the problems.

The sixth group used a grid based on multiples of fifteen. This group was the smallest, and they worked from a problem set focused on three digit addition.

Although the groups had slight variations in size, there were four active roles for students in the groups:

1. Calculator—counts the pips on the dice, or computes the solution to the problem on the sheet. This student talks through her process aloud as she works.
2. Verifier—checks the math problem and is available to help in the computation process.
3. Programmer—writes and inputs the program needed to navigate the robot to the solution.
4. Debugger—follows the program as it runs to discover any errors; also available to assist in the programming process.

When Tali introduced the lesson, she spent time talking about each of the roles. Then a group including Tali role-played through a turn, rotation, and a second turn. This modeled each role as well as the process of changing roles. Compared to managing role rotation, programming a robot is easy. This was not the first lesson using robots for these students. Almost all of the students were very comfortable with the Bee-Bots. Most of the direct instruction in this lesson was about how to talk to your group members—how to ask for help, how to offer help, and how to decline help.

Once the students were assigned roles and allowed to begin, they worked for about twelve minutes before Tali paused the class for reflection. She asked students to share "what they had noticed" so far. This group reflection allows students to share their experience, thus developing an understanding that others in the room are having an experience similar to their own. Toward the end of this time, the group working on three digit addition asked for a second sheet of challenges.

The number grids and problem sheets do require some work to prep. If you have a poster board and access to a lamination machine, you can easily create reusable grids. With masking tape, you could also create a grid directly on the floor or the tabletop.

This lesson is a good example of robot-as-pointer. The answers are on the grid, and you program the robot to go to the answer. The activity helps develop literacy skills associated with sequencing, but beyond that the real learning potential is in the communication needed to manage the four roles and to rotate through those roles. The lesson also provides models of differentiation applied to technology class. This model only differentiates on the math challenge, even though the stated learning goals are social.

How can robot-as-pointer be adapted to other content areas?

1. Navigate to the first and last letter sounds in a word.
2. Fly to the planets in order.
3. Go to the right place in a neighborhood to buy fresh fruit.

This type of lesson works well with pre-K through first-grade students. Each robot moves slowly and only a short distance. It is very easy for the students to figure out how many steps the Bee-Bot needs to take. Every step is the length of one Bee-Bot.

The instructional model "robot-as-pointer" applies to other robots. Older students will be very successful using Sphero's SPRK program to control the Sphero robots. These quick little robots need more room to run, so place the answers around the room. Tickle app is an amazing programming platform that makes it easy for second graders to drive Dash around the room and record amazing sounds with Dot.

Does your school have an amazing robot-friendly outdoor space? Before you rush out to play, here are some things to do and consider:

1. Are your devices protected? (with a strong case and screen insurance)
2. Do the robots work on the surface? The concrete might be too smooth, or the grass might be too long. You are going to have to test it out first. It might look like you are playing with robots, but you are researching learning conditions.
3. Are your kids conscientious? Make sure that the outdoor learning you are considering won't be completely distracting to other classes in the area. Ask them for help in taking care of the robots and devices.

If the answer to any of these questions is no, consider taking over part of the gym if you can get away with it.

ROBOT-AS-CONSTANT

Robots used in a lesson should be used to their full potential. What does a robot do? Exactly what you tell it to do. Pedagogically, to capitalize on this, think about the robot serving the role of "constant" in an experiment. Ask a robot to roll forward at fifty percent power for two seconds and that is exactly what it will do. How far will it go? That depends on many things outside of the robot and its programming. This space, just outside of the robot and its programming, is where teachers build the learning experience.

The lesson in this example is from second grade. Danielle and Diana, the second-grade team, were looking for a new way to learn about forces. They were just beginning to adjust their scope and sequence to align more closely with the Next Generation Science Standards. Robots can be a great way to create a hands-on learning experience; and working with their STEM coordinator, Megan, the second-grade team decided to introduce inclined planes using Sphero robots.

This lesson was a true introduction, with very brief direct instruction focused on the term "inclined plane" and what it means. The learning objectives for this lesson were as follows:

1. Discover and observe the qualities of different inclined planes.
2. Describe the qualities of an inclined plane.

The lesson was a loose rotation through learning stations. Activity centers were set up in a large open room. Each center was designed to support a short task. In some cases, the task is a question they need to answer or something they need to do and observe. In the case of this lesson on inclined planes, each station was a ramp or inclined plane of a different length and pitch.

Students were paired up, and each pair had an iPad, a Sphero robot, a small whiteboard, and a block. The pairs were asked to use their robot to explore the various inclined planes. The tech specialist programmed the robots in Tickle to a set speed and time. The program constrained the robots to fifty percent speed for three seconds. This program supported the role of "Robot-as-constant." The students were asked not to alter the program for the first half of the in-class exploration.

There were four different stations, each set up to accommodate three pairs of students, and students were encouraged to explore them freely. Some teachers might need to set up times for the rotations. In this lesson, the teacher occasionally reminded students to switch roles often and visit all of the stations. Students were also encouraged to use the whiteboard as an adjustable ramp, and they explored how adding a shallow pitched plane to a steeply pitched plane changed how far up the ramp the robot could run.

After students progressed through each of the four stations, the students created a narrated photo reflection. In this case, they used the app Puppet Pals HD Director's Pass to import a photo of their robot on an inclined plane and record a description of what they learned and observed. The videos were less than a minute long and were uploaded directly to the student work blog as a summative assessment.

In their exploration, the second-grade scientists discovered more than the teachers planned for or hoped. The teacher hoped that students would figure out that the steeper ramp required more energy to climb. What they did not anticipate was that the students would lay one ramp atop the other. The students were working on solving the problem, "How to get the robot the furthest up the ramp." As an introduction to inclined planes, this lesson was very successful, and most of the students had a very good practical understanding of inclined planes at the end of class.

Robot-as-constant is not the most adaptable of the strategies. It works well for young children learning about friction and observing that the robots run differently on different surfaces. If you are using a waterproof robot like Sphero, you may be able to explore properties of liquids also. The focus of these lessons is not the robot, but the world it moves through.

ROBOT-AS-ACTOR

A robot in the classroom can be a simple programmable puppet. Students can program a robot to move, act, and even speak. When students use robots as actors, it frees them from the pressure of performance and makes the cognitive task more complex.

A robot is a physical avatar; it stands in for someone. These programmable actors have been standing in for people in assembly lines and factories for years. Some robots can broadcast recorded sound or adjust their "mood" through color and sound. Cute and expressive robots are very engaging for children. Teachers can capitalize on this natural engagement by adding robots to previous "make a skit" activities.

Narrative and programming both rely on sequence. When students write a program that instructs a robot to reenact a narrative, they are doing a very complex sequencing task. In fact, the task is considerably more complex than simply writing the narrative or writing the program. When students are asked to work together to program a robot to act out a narrative sequence, they are engaged in complex learning.

The lesson in this chapter is almost ready to go; it is only missing a central text that the students will be retelling. The lesson uses the Dash and Dot robots from Wonder Workshop, programmed through the iPad app Blockly. For students who are not yet reading, this lesson can use the Path app with limited functionality and an even larger role for imaginative play.

Teachers can present this literary lesson to the students as a movie-making experience. In groups of three to five, students will write a short scene, program a robot to act out the scripted scene, and get help from their group in filming their short scene. Then the group will combine each scene into a movie.

The Learning Objectives

1. Students will practice retelling a story with a clear beginning, middle, and end.
2. Students will program a robot to follow scripted commands.
3. Students will collaborate with a small group on authorship and production of a short video.

Working in Groups

This lesson is designed to be part of a multiweek unit focused on a single subject or author. The activities are planned out to be delivered as three forty-five-minute weekly classes. The tricky balance is allowing the students enough time to write, script, program, and film without succumbing to the impulse to give them all the time they need. Without a meaningful deadline, students will not learn how to manage time or make the call that something is "good enough." Giving them all the time they need will not make their films great—possibly not even better than they would be when created in a constrained time situation.

Students need enough time to:

1. Write a thirty-second scene with detailed actions for Dash.
2. Program Dash to act out the scene.
3. Test the program with Dash.
4. Work with their group to get scenes filmed.
5. Record voice-over if needed.
6. Compile and export video.

This lesson works well with groups of three, but it can be adapted to fit groups of four to five. When adding group members, be sure to add more time. Programming the robot is not simple, and the lesson as written does put a bit of pressure on groups of three. Students could engage in managed roles, but then some would spend most of their time filming and might not write or program. With a class of twenty-four students, eight robots would be a great number for a class set. With fewer than eight robots, the lesson would need to be simplified or extended into four class sessions.

This lesson is not designed to introduce the programming of the Dash robot, nor is it designed to teach students how to record a movie on a tablet. These are foundational skills that need their own time. When students are working on a complex project like this over several class periods, management of time and resources can be challenging. Here are some tips:

1. Set a two-take max on video shoots. Endless retakes are not allowed. Try your best, try again, and move on.
2. Have students share their program directly via e-mail.
3. Reward good code. When students figure out a good way to do something, share that out. Support a culture of collaborative learning.
4. Set time limits on robot program testing. Be prepared to help students manage turns.

5. Make sure students have scripts and programs written before they even have a robot in hand.
6. The students should know the robots before using them in a lesson like this. To be prepared for success in this lesson, students should have at least an hour of hands-on experience with the robots and the programming apps.
7. This lesson model adapts well to any summary activity. Students can write a book trailer starring Dash and Dot, or retell any important story studied in class.

This lesson provides many opportunities to support students. The best support available for students in a lesson like this is a functional group. The right group for an activity like this is a mix of abilities and egos. A lesson that uses imaginative play to bridge the gap between the remembered story and the script asks students to take creative risks. A collaborative learning community is the best support teachers can provide for these creative risks. When possible, teachers should place students in groups they feel support them.

Starter programs can be important support pieces in any programming class. The teacher builds a program that has all of the needed pieces for success. Students who need more support can download the starter program and remix it. In real-world programming, people use code libraries all the time; take a moment and browse the GitHub website. More than any other field, programming depends on collaboration. GitHub and other cloud-based code libraries are user-generated resources; programmers use code from the library, and, when they write an original piece that might be useful to others, they post it.

Pace and Structure

This robot and narrative unit has several significant pieces and spans at least three class periods. A lesson this complex requires both careful planning and flexibility. In addition to managing all of the tasks involved, the teacher's greatest challenge is toeing the pedagogical line. Can even this lesson be empowering to students? Can choice be protected in the process?

Group work employs both choice and compromise. Each group's movie will need three representative scenes. There needs to be a beginning, middle, and end. Within those demands, students can choose. As the groups plan their scenes, be sure to check in and help them make great choices.

In this assignment, students are asked to write and program their scene. They are working with groups to create a short retelling of a text being studied in the class. The first negotiation in the group was about who would write which scene (beginning, middle, and end). Once that was settled, the students set to scripting. By working out who would cover which part of the film first, this group maintained choice. Each of the students made their decision about what to include in their scene, and then passed on their assigned segment.

No robots are out at this point. The robots only arrive once students have a script and a first draft of their program. Often this will not happen until the second class.

Day One

1. Student scripts a scene, which include blocking notes for the robot's actions.
2. Using Tickle app or Blockly, student drafts a program of the full scene.

Day Two

3. Student sets the stage for the filming.
4. Student gets a robot and tests the program, debugging as needed.
5. Student works with a partner to film the robot performing the scene.

Day Three

6. Student shares the film with group members in a Google Drive folder or using Airdrop.
7. Student writes voice-over script (if needed).
8. Group works together to edit and produce the summary movie.

In many ways, "Robot-as-actor" is a very adaptable role. The lesson described here has been used in second and fourth grades. Below second grade, this lesson requires adjustment to keep the focus on the content-area learning. The programming platforms used here, Tickle app and Blockly, require basic reading skills. When this lesson was used in kindergarten, the teachers used the KIBO robot. KIBO uses a programming interface built out of wooden blocks.

The kindergarten students were very successful stringing wood blocks together to write the program, and then using the barcode scanner on the robot to input the program. Marina Bers is one of the designers of the KIBO robot and the wooden block interface. Her ideas about play and learning connect all the way back to John Locke in 1693, the first recorded use or mention of alphabet blocks. Bers makes the challenge of syntax purely physical and there is almost nothing abstact about the robot-student interaction.

The kindergarten students programmed the robot to act out important pieces of their Jewish identity. The robots acted out lighting candles, dancing, and singing. When students program a robot to do something about the subject they have been studying, they have to slow down and think carefully about procedure and sequence. In the case of the kindergarten students, they deconstructed actions like lighting candles into a sequence of movements that they programmed into a robot. The robot supports learning by adding a layer of procedural thinking and problem solving to almost any assignment.

Robot as Innovation Engine

Most of the robots discussed so far have been wheeled wonders zipping across the floor, many with cute light-up eyes. These roots are hardly representative of the robots in our lives. Our garage door opener doesn't carry the weight of personality, but it is a very simple programmable machine. Robots are programmable machines, and, in schools, robots can be used to teach about designing programmable machines.

From lights to thermostats, we live in an increasingly programmable world. Students need to be prepared to interact with programmable machines at the designer level. There are several great options for teachers looking to get students designing and prototyping.

1. Modular Robotics
2. Lego WeDo
3. Thymio
4. Hummingbird
5. Raspberry PI

Modular Robotics (http://www.modrobotics.com/)

The Cubelets and MOSS robot building systems from Modular Robotics are the precursor to the amazing NAO robots in *Big Hero 6*. The Cubelets robots allow students as young as four to discover, program, and create by connecting preprogrammed blocks. The small plastic blocks are the programming interface; they do not connect to computers or tablets. The physical blocks can snap together to connect a power source to a sensor and a buzzer or make a light dependent on a motion sensor or a motor respond to sound. When students need more functionality and mobility, they can graduate from the Cubelets robots to the MOSS robotics kits.

Lego WeDo (http://wiki.scratch.mit.edu/wiki/LEGO%C2%
AE_WeDo%E2%84%A2_Construction_Set)

Lego WeDo is a small kit of motors and sensors that allow students to construct programmable LEGO projects. The main control block connects via USB to a computer running either the native Lego WeDo program or Scratch 2.0. The programming platform that ships with WeDo has very little text and can be used by prereading students who know how to use a mouse to control a conventional computer.

Thymio (http://www.techykids.com)

The Thymio robot is a self-contained robot with two motors, twenty sensors, and Lego-compatible build points. The robot has several preprogrammed modes allowing for discovery-based learning. The robot connects via USB to a conventional computer for programming. With a flexible programming interface that employs both visual and text-based programming, Thymio supports programmers from prereading through early high school.

Hummingbird (http://www.hummingbirdkit.com/)

The Hummingbird robotics building system is marketed as an imagination engine. Students who are confident readers can use this kit to combine motors, lights, sensors, and switches with cardboard boxes and construction paper to create awesome animatronic projects. The sensors are connected to an Arduino-style microcontroller that plugs into a conventional computer. The kit is programmed with Scratch. This is a great tool to scaffold up to independent design with Arduinos in later grades.

Raspberry PI (https://www.raspberrypi.org/blog/tag/education/)

The Raspberry PI is a complete computer that students can use at the center of an innovation and design project. The PI is the interface. Students need a screen and a keyboard, but no other computer. The potential for designing with Raspberry PI is seemingly limitless. It can be used for conventional programming, or it can be turned into a robot. Read through some of the work other teachers have done with the PI, and you will be surprised about the full text programming some teachers have been able to support in students as young as first grade.

The Road to Innovation

It is beyond the scope of this simple survey to suggest how to set up an innovation class, especially for elementary grades. The ideal innovation class for younger students might be a balance between the structure and project management Don Wettrick presents in *Pure Genius* and Sharon Marzouk's work supporting student innovation in afterschool and summer programs.

Students in my colleague Sharon's afterschool program engage in design thinking to create a project that responds to a real need and uses a Thymio robot as an element of design. The Thymio has built-in sensors as well as strategic build points that allow users to connect it to LEGO bricks.

The tools exist to bring rapid prototyping to the classroom. More than ever before, teachers can support students by providing the tools needed for students to design real solutions to real problems. When teachers match the available tools with a dedication to student choice, the potential for engaged and relevant learning is overwhelming. Without proper planning and support, these same tools can turn into a craft factory turning out twenty-four Bluetooth birdhouses before Mother's Day.

Programming sensors to collect data and programming motors to run in response to that data is the very heart of robotics. Designing tools that apply this functionality engage computational thinking and problem solving.

Students of any age can design a tool or device to solve a problem. Supporting students in this adventure requires a good match between the student's reading level and the programming platform. Some of the tools, like the LEGO WeDo and the Thymio robot, offer a range of programming interfaces. Multiple interfaces make it easier to craft a range of lessons and supports, and this in turn increases the range of ages the robot can effectively engage.

The robots in which you and your school choose to invest will make some integration choices for you. Some robots swim, others draw. Which robots are best for your school? As there are new robots coming out every day, any recommendation in this text would quickly become dated. Here are some key factors to consider:

1. Total cost. This is the cost of the robots plus any devices you will need to support the robots, plus the cost of maintenance and repair. (Plan on a thirty percent breakage and failure for robots that see heavy use.)
2. Figure out the per-user cost. Take your total cost and divide by the number of users the robots will likely see. Can the robots be shared across a grade level? Would storing robots at a resource center get them into more classrooms? If three classes of twenty-four students share one twelve-robot class set of Spheros, the total cost of $3600 (twelve Spheros at $1200 plus twelve Android tablets at $2400), divided by the seventy-two students in the three combined classes, means the per-user cost is $50.
3. Think about the space available. Fast robots need more space than slower robots. Can the tables and chairs in the classroom be easily moved?

Do teachers at the school site have easy access to a large open space? Thinking realistically about the space you have to work in can help make the choice between a robot that slowly steps 15 cm at a time and a turbo-powered coffee can that zips at fourteen miles an hour.

4. Control. A quality programming interface can support learning even more than the robot itself. Robots in the classroom should be programmable by a variety of apps appropriate to a wide range of ages. The Tickle app is currently an industry leader in connecting to a wide range of classroom-level robots. Tickle helps students master the Internet of things. From Hue lighting to Ollie, Sphero, Dash and Dot, the Tickle app lets students use familiar block-based programming to control the world around them. In addition to supporting third-party programming, an educational robot should have at least two programming interfaces of its own, as well as a simple remote control mode. At least one of the programming apps should be focused on graphical input, like Sphero's Draw N' Drive or Wonder Workshop's Path.

Chapter 8

Programming to Learn Social Skills

With thoughtful planning, any lesson can be constructed to support developing social and emotional skills. In this chapter, we will explore designing learning experiences that use the high-engagement tools of programming apps and robots to help students learn to work together and communicate.

Some of the ideas in this chapter will run counter to current conventional wisdom and what some view as the traditional role of teachers. You will be asked to consider teaching less, to explore the power of underinstruction, to leave more room for student discovery. If you are proud of your 1:1 program, you will be challenged to underdeploy devices to create more opportunities for students to learn with each other. Even in a setting with a screen for every student, making strategic choices about pair programming can have a profound impact on your ability to meet social and emotional learning (SEL) goals.

Collaboration, whether in pairs or groups of five, provides the opportunity to teach social skills and requires students to use their social and emotional skills. The high-engagement nature and game-like design of programming apps and robots are an invitation to teachers. High-engagement tools invite teachers to pile on high-challenge learning goals.

Teachers are always teaching the visible curriculum as well as ongoing lessons about learning and working with others. One of the joys of elementary education is the ability to focus directly on communication, self-awareness, and social skills.

Sharing Is Hard

When working on social and emotional skills, body language is a great data point. Are students relaxed? Start with a baseline. The first time you hand a tablet to students, watch how they take it and what they do next. It is not uncommon to see students draw the device close to them and turn away from other students. They claim the device as their own and are ready to defend their right to that device. If the class goals are cooperation and teamwork, this is a meaningful, if not encouraging, baseline for growth.

When we ask students to work together on a device, the sharing we model for them must be more than taking turns. Learning is not a roller coaster, and we don't have the time to make anyone wait to learn. If we put two students on one iPad, we must also give each student an active role to play at all times. No matter the objectives of the lesson plan, teachers are always engaged in covert instruction. Even though we may not set aside a day for character education, teachers are always helping students understand what it means to be kind or nice.

A student working alone at a device will not learn much about social skills. Unlike the deeply embedded connection of programming to literacy, logic, and math, there is no magical relationship between programming and playing nice. Fortunately, teachers can intentionally construct the learning context to serve some robust SEL goals.

PAIRED PROGRAMMING FOR THE WIN

The educational world is very excited about 1:1 programs, and not without reason. Even when an iPad is available for every student, strategically under-deploying devices opens new opportunities to meet SEL goals. Although it is challenging to put more than two students on a tablet, due to the size of the device, there is amazing work students can do as a pair. Paired programming is much more than taking turns; when we work together, we can develop communication and problem-solving skills.

Introducing a leveled app to kindergarten students is a great opportunity to use paired programming to develop communication skills. For this lesson, the objective set by the classroom teacher was problem solving and turn taking. The teachers worked together to develop some sentence starters for offering to help: "Do you need help?" and "Can I help?" They also helped the students accept and decline help with, "Yes, please" and "No, I would like to try to figure this out."

We are always teaching problem solving, and Kodable gives students a series of appropriately complex, yet small, problems to solve. This supplies a high-engagement platform for teaching social skills. Both students want to solve each problem, so it can be challenging to keep the focus cooperative.

When the teachers modeled turn taking, they were sure to define the length of one turn. They made sure to use a level as a turn, an appropriate in-app goal. If time is used to define a turn, the student waiting will only watch the time. The hands-off partner is mentally rehearsing the coding activity, while the hands-on partner moves the pieces into their places.

Step by Step—Building an SEL Lesson in Kindergarten

What does it take to teach sharing in an active way? For the example social emotional learning lesson, we will focus on kindergarten, fairly early in the year. In the planning stage of the lesson, set an ambitious goal. A programming lesson is going to use unique tools, even if you are teaching an off-line lesson. Capitalize on your high-engagement tools by setting truly ambitious goals.

For this lesson, a technology specialist was collaborating with the general studies teacher. The greatest challenge this early in the year, as identified by the teachers, was sharing and communication. Working together, the team set a few specific learning goals:

1. Students will learn and practice communication strategies.
2. Students will collaborate to solve problems.
3. Students will practice sharing and turn taking.

With these goals set, the technology teacher found a supporting tool and deployment model. In this case, the tool was the programming app Kodable, and the deployment model was pair programming. Pair programming is a good fit for these goals, because it puts students elbow to elbow and knee to knee on one device. So whatever the students are doing, it should be challenging enough that they will need to work together to solve some problems.

Since this was early in the year, the tech teacher used this as a lesson to introduce Kodable, a leveled programming app. The levels made it easy for the students to understand when their turn as programmer had ended, and the levels were challenging enough that most students genuinely needed to talk through the solutions with their partner to be successful.

In a technology class that is only forty-five minutes long, there can be pressure to get the kids working, but before they get the iPads, they get the lesson. The lesson in this case was about communication and problem solving.

Since lecture is a challenging mode in which to learn about communication, role-playing is recommended. In this lesson, two teachers role-played working together, stopping the role-play to ask students questions. The goal of the role-play was to get kids thinking about working with their partner. The points of focus were as follows:

1. Asking your partner for help.
2. Offering help to a partner.
3. Declining help from your partner.

Asking for Help

We want the students to learn a few things when they are asking for help. They need to know that everyone asks for help, that their classmate can be a great resource, and that waiting for a teacher is not always the best strategy. We model simple communication: "Can you help me figure this out?" or "What would you do to solve this problem?" Both engage the partner in learning and help them to know their role. In addition to talking about what the person asking for help says, teachers should help students think through how to best help. If you only want one rule to guide the interaction, here it is: the person helping cannot touch the iPad.

Offering Help to a Partner

Working in pairs can be very challenging, especially if students see their partners struggling and want to help. Students need to see this in action. In the role-play, be sure to highlight the process of waiting long enough before offering help, and then show them how to offer help. If the students were reading, we could post these prompts on the board and have a broader range, but for the early part of the year, the simplicity of communication is important. The offer needs to be kind and respectful, which is mostly in tone. The words, "You look like you could use some help with that, can I help?" work very well, and students will adapt it slightly as they become more comfortable. As teachers role-play for the students, they might talk about both their feelings and how they are acting on those feelings.

Declining Help from Your Partner

When we are learning about programming, we know that we will have to try things many times before they work. The students share their challenge points and ask each other for help often. One of the great skills you can give students is the ability to thank someone they are turning down. When a student offers help, and the struggling student is not yet ready to accept help, they can look up at their partner and say, "Thanks for your offer, but I want to try at this for a bit longer." This acknowledges the partner and their value, while focusing on the importance of struggling through this problem. Even when help is offered and needed, the rule applies; only the student whose turn it is can touch the iPad, and the other partner can only talk them through it.

ENGINEERING SOCIAL CHALLENGES

When you want to support students' social skill development, it is important to construct safe and challenging social learning environments. Technology can be very social, but most end user devices like tablets or laptops are optimized for one person. Tablets like iPads were designed as a single-user device. About the same size as a sheet of paper, they are half the size of an open textbook. They are not designed for sharing. That is the very reason they are a great tool for teaching communication and sharing. Teachers need instructional models to support kids collaborating on devices; these models need to support both content-area and social skills learning goals.

Learning Stations

In situations that have two or more students to each iPad, learning stations leverage hybrid learning strategies and student choice to support engaged independent work. Learning stations can be organized as a whole class activity or as a drop-in center for students who finish work early.

Tips for Whole Class Learning Stations

The secret to whole class learning stations is managed scarcity. Even in situations where you could deploy an iPad to each student, in learning stations you only deploy as many iPads as you need to satisfy the active roles.

1. No waiting. The classroom is not a theme park; we do not wait to learn. Make sure each role in the group is active.
2. Define a turn clearly. Make it easy for all kids in the room to know when they should rotate roles.
3. Model turn management. When you first use groups and stations, model and role-play turn management. Students need to see the process work.
4. Not every station has to have tech, but every station has to have enough active roles.
5. Use tech differently at different stations. At one station the iPad might be just data collection or reflection; at another it might be used to program a robot to complete a challenge.
6. Build choice in whenever possible. If you have six groups, develop eight stations and ask the students to get to six. This requires them to make choices and be aware of other groups.
7. If you are teaching social skills and communication, don't design all the conflict out of the lesson. Choice may complicate things, but consider that each slight conflict is an opportunity to practice the communication skills at the heart of the lesson.
8. Not all students have to make it to all stations. Consider timing the stations for one or two rotations, and keep track of which groups completed which stations.

Choice Time and Challenge Cards

Robots and iPads can be a powerful draw during choice time. Students want to have extracurricular time with these tools; they want to play. Teachers can capitalize on this engagement and put reasonable limits on the play through challenge cards. A teacher might say that the robots are available, but only if a student is working on a challenge. Each challenge card will have a simple (or not) robot-based challenge and requirements. One of the requirements would be for three team members. Perhaps other challenges only have two needed team members, but the more enticing the challenge, the bigger the possible team.

Challenge cards are simply goals and challenges written out on cards so the students can just grab a card, put a team together, and get the equipment. What can be on the challenge cards?

- Design a chariot your robot can pull.
- Create a story acted out by two robots.
- Robot joust! Design jousting gear for two robots and program them to joust.
- Power climb! Build a giant hill that a robot can climb.
- Interpretive dance party. Program dancing robots.

The importance is not so much the exact activity, but that the activity is rich enough that there are many decisions the group must reach agreement on. There should also be enough to do without the robot that no one is waiting to drive the robot, but everyone is paying close attention to whose turn it is.

Chapter 9

Programming to Learn to Read

Literacy is a vital and important mission of education. The earlier the students get interested in reading and feel successful at reading, the better they do in school. Creating a text-rich coding lesson begins with the lessons you are already using in class. Don't throw away the planning and lesson design you've already done. Instead, ask yourself, "What happens if I move this activity off of a piece of paper and into a programming environment?" Word ladders are great activities for helping students to see how words and sounds are related as well as to practice spelling. But how would you transform a word ladder worksheet into a digital learning lesson?

In an open studio app like ScratchJr, you can create a simple spelling activity in just a few steps. Let's start very simply and ask students to spell a common sight word. After we look at designing a program for one word, we will walk through how to build up to word ladders.

Preparing to Code to Learn

Before you can code to learn with your students, they do need to learn to use a programming app. Before using an open studio app for a content-rich lesson, use leveled apps to help your students develop an understanding of what they can do in a programming app. When we are using coding to learn, the challenge has to be the content we want students to learn and not the programming platform itself. If the students find the platform too difficult or distracting, you would be better off running off some copies of the blackline masters and dusting off the overhead projector. The goal is that digital lesson design be as reliable as the overhead and easier than whiteout.

Creating content-rich lessons inside of a programming environment like Hopscotch or ScratchJr asks students to work with content while also developing their understanding of sequence and syntax. We are talking about a lesson that is not alongside an app, but inside it.

Fundamentals of Digital Lesson Design for Literacy

As more tablets enter classrooms, more teachers are challenged to engage in digital lesson design. Some teachers have decades of experience creating analog, paper-based learning activities. Many teachers spent years learning all of the formatting and layout possibilities of Microsoft Word or Adobe Pagemaker. Now comes a new challenge, paired with an opportunity. Designing lessons for tablets is more complex than changing the export format on the desktop publishing software.

Tablets are more interactive than paper; the challenge is to determine the most pedagogically powerful tools inside of this amazing machine. What can teachers ask of their students now that they have access to a digital personal assistant? Designing lessons for devices requires teachers to make the same thoughtful decisions about how and what to teach, but the how is more complex than it once was. How will work be created and shared? If every student has access to a camera, what opportunities for learning does that open up?

Programming requires students and teachers to develop their understanding of programming while they are already programming. Like on-the-job training, the content teaches you a great deal about how to do things. But once you have bought into the idea that learning experiences can be built around programming activities, how do you plan that lesson?

High-Engagement Platforms Demand High-Value Goals

Programming on iPads and robots is something students look forward to, and teachers can capitalize on that. Match high-challenge learning goals with the high-engagement tools of programming and robots. Designing lessons for a new learning medium creates many opportunities for innovation, so start with your highest goals. What is the most important lesson? Which lesson do you struggle to support? Once you have a goal selected, you have to build the activity to meet the goal.

Literacy First Lesson Design

When you make a paper handout for your students, how do you give them directions? How would that change if you could record your voice saying the directions? At each point in the process, think about the features of the programming platform. In ScratchJr, there is an audio record function, so you could build a button that, when pressed, plays a recorded message, possibly directions or a hint.

When you are designing a literacy lesson think carefully about how ready your students are to read directions, and then don't explain any directions you have written. One of the most valuable skills we are always practicing is how to read a screen. When you are designing a lesson, think about how you can use the screen to communicate. You can label objects, or even have characters speak in comic-style speech bubbles. Spend some time in apps like The Foos, Tynker, and Kodable, and look for how the apps offer support and tips. The more confident your readers, the more written instructions and support you should build into the lessons.

Once you have created the embedded instructions, don't explain them out loud. Teaching students to read requires us to construct situations where reading is rewarding. When students don't know what to do and they ask their teacher, the teacher can either answer the question directly or help shape the problem-solving strategy the student is using. In this case, redirecting the student to read the directions asks the student to apply the very skills you are looking to develop.

Is the best mode of instruction for your students direct demonstration? Use a program like Reflector or ScreenChomp to make a screencast of your tablet, provide a voice-over, and demonstrate the skill or activity. During the lesson, make sure the link is available to students so that they can watch it again if they need to. Experiment with playing a movie instead of live demonstration, and see if it works for your students.

Differentiation

Differentiation in tablet-based instruction is completely possible, and it does require some information about students' current reading ability. If you are lucky enough to be working with another teacher in this project, make sure each of you have a good understanding of how much support individual students need. If this information is not available before the lesson, as it sometimes happens, you need to design a learning experience with a variety of options and challenges.

The goal of differentiation is to provide an appropriate challenge to each student to support their learning. For some students, this will mean introducing more scaffolding into the lesson; for others, ensuring the activity has several advanced challenges available.

Scaffolding in programming can take many forms. The first is a good model text. This model text is a piece of code that works, something that meets the minimum requirement of the challenge. If you are asking students to line letters up to spell a word, you might give them the code for the first letter so they have it as a resource. Resource code is a real thing in the world of programming. There are actually online banks of functional code that programmers can use as a basis for whatever they are trying to do. Resource code is also different from giving students the answer. If you give the students too much, many will wait for you to give them the solution. So if the students struggle with programming, give them the full code for one letter and talk with them about why the code works. Then click over to a different letter and ask them how the code should begin.

Differentiation in either direction needs a human component. As described above, the code support is a resource that becomes actively useful when someone talks through the code with the student. The best case is that this helper is someone who knows how to avoid overhelping. Teachers always walk a balance between helping a student succeed on the task at hand and supporting lifelong success. I believe teachers have to support students in discovering things for themselves, and sometimes this means not answering questions you think they can figure out. The key is to provide enough information to get them thinking, and then to ask the question that gets them coding.

The Open-Ended Challenge, the Top End of Differentiation

A well-designed lesson in any media is going to be accessible to every student and has plenty of built-in challenges. While we can plan well for the students who need help reading or sequencing, it can be a much greater challenge to plan for the students that will move through the lesson quickly and with a great deal of success. Some of these students will devour your lesson, and be truly engaged in the activity, but they complete the assigned task and their first question is, "What's Next?"

A great advantage to designing a code-centered literacy lesson in an open studio app like ScratchJr is that students can also create activities. In the lessons below, notice the extension activities. When I create a lesson, I always plan two or three extension activities to keep my fastest kids engaged and challenged. These activities tend to fall into following types:

1. Repeat the main activity using more advanced programming.
2. Design a new level of the activity.
3. Share your layer with a classmate and play it with them.

Assessment

Two of the advantages of leveled apps, like Kodable, The Foos, and the play side of the Tynker app, are the built-in verification and engagement tools. The verification gives the students real-time feedback at the end of the level and then allows them to try to complete the level again if they want to improve their score. At the end of the lesson, the teacher can look at the app or onto a master teacher dashboard on the web interface to see how well each student did and how far they got in the game. The engagement tools are the coins, stars, happy sounds and, in the case of The Foos, the dance of celebration. These serve as cheerleaders to the students and help keep them interested in solving the challenges put forward in the app.

While there are ways to create these things in an open studio app, the process is time consuming, and the output is not the most usable information. When designing a digital learning experience, don't hesitate to adapt a traditional assessment to fit the lesson. The most important thing is to think about your learning goals and make sure your assessments actually give you information about whether or not the students met the goals.

Use the tablet to create and share data. Can your students create a screenshot on their tablet? Most devices have a screenshot trigger that involves pushing two buttons at once. This is a skill that comes easily to many first grade students and most second grade students. Once the students take a screenshot, they can e-mail it to the teacher or to the class blog, or submit it to a shared Google drive folder. They can also add another layer of information by narrating over their screenshot for a "Code Talk." Think of this as a running record for programming using iMovie, Puppet Pals Director's Pass, Fotobabble, Explain Everything, or any of a multitude of video or presentation creation tools. Once they make a very short video (limit them to a minute), they can post it to Google Drive or e-mail it to the class blog.

Assessment can be a group share-out and reflection at the end of the lesson or even short "What are you learning?" breaks. Ask students to put devices face down, and then ask a few to share what they are learning so far. Pairing this with critically watching them work can be a good mix. It is challenging to rely on over-the-shoulder assessments, because often when you would like to be assessing students, there are others that require direct help. You can also have them post what they are learning to the class blog.

Guided Access

Up until this point we have talked about what a teacher can add to an open studio app like ScratchJr to support student success. We have mentioned instructions and help buttons and even touched on strategies for exporting work for assessment. In designing the learning experience, teachers can also keep the lesson on target by removing some components of the open studio app. By using Guided Access on the iPad, you can define and disable parts of the screen. This is important for the youngest students, simply because it disables the home button, keeping them in the app.

In ScratchJr, there are some helpful buttons to disable:

1. The on-screen home button in the upper left
2. The backgrounds button in the top center
3. The add character button in the left column
4. The add scene button in the right column.

Also be clear with the students when you are giving directions that they are not to be editing or coloring characters. There are simply too many paths into the edit character mode to disable all of the buttons.

The most important area to turn off is the main stage. If you are asking students to use programming to move letters into order, be sure they cannot just click and drag the letters into position by turning off the main stage. If you want students to do something in a challenging way, do not leave an easier way open to them. In the case of moving letters on the screen, you would still be meeting the literacy goals, but the sequencing and programming would be left behind. What we want is a spiral of reinforcing skills with sequencing in both the coding and the spelling.

Step by Step—How to Build Your First Lesson in ScratchJr

The goal for this tutorial is to provide a clear walk through the entire process of making a lesson in ScratchJr for kindergarten or first grade students. As with any instructions, if your device has different buttons or options, focus on what is being done, and employ YouTube or the app developers' website to discover how to do it.

The learning goal for this lesson is to have the students use programming to spell a four-letter sight word. This lesson is designed to be completed by a single student but can easily be adapted to pair programming. If you have a device with ScratchJr, please follow the directions and try creating your own lesson. Your goal in completing this is to become familiar with the interface. We have set a learning objective; now we will begin to add elements to the program. In general, the elements are nonmoving background images or moving sprites. Both backgrounds and sprites can be controlled by programming within the app.

For this lesson, we are going to add a background image of a line and four sprites, one for each letter of the sight word.

1. Turn on the Grid.
   After opening the app and selecting a new project, turn on the grid button above the stage on the left, next to the full screen button. This grid will

help you align the elements in your program so the letters actually sit directly on the line. It is very important for students that the letter touches the line—so important that it can derail a lesson if a student cannot make it line up.

2. Create Target Line as Background Image.

Press the background button, which is top center left above the stage and looks like a landscape. With none of the backgrounds selected, press the paintbrush button in the upper right-hand corner. Choose a color for your line by clicking on the color on the bottom of the screen. Using the grid as a guide, draw a line on the second grid line up from the bottom of the stage. If you are not satisfied with your line, use the undo button in the upper left to erase it, and try again. There are on-screen settings for line width. Once you are pleased with your line, click the check mark in the upper right-hand corner.

3. Create Sprites.

Before we create the four sprites we need for our sight word, we have to delete the cat. Click and hold on the cat character until it begins wobbling. Once the cat is wobbling, you should be able to click on a white "x" icon to delete the sprite.

To create a new sprite, click the plus sign in the column to the left of the stage. Without selecting any character on the screen, tap the paintbrush button in the upper right. Draw the letter in a two-by-two piece of the grid. Be consistent with the size to avoid alignment issues when the students are programming. Be sure to carefully model the letters using the handwriting method your school practices. Once the letter is complete, press the check mark in the upper right-hand corner.

For this lesson, we are going to use the sight word "LOVE." Create the four letters in order, left to right; while their order can be scrambled on the stage, in the left-hand column, the word will be in order. This is a nice contextual support for the students.

4. Code the First Letter.

Once you have the letters created as sprites and the line drawn on the background, move all the letters to the top of the screen. You can put all the letters on the same line if you want to make the programming a little easier. Now you are ready to write the starter code. This is the sample code you send to the students to give them a reference to use as they write the rest of the code.

Select the "L" character by clicking on it in the left-hand column. Make sure you have the grid button activated. This will show you which block is being used to locate your sprite. If the L is at (3, 13), listing the X or across dimension first, and the line is located at three up from the bottom (3, 03) the L needs to move down ten spaces.

From the yellow menu, select the yellow block with the green flag. Drag this block into the program area at the bottom of the screen.

Press the blue menu button, and from the movement menu select the down arrow. Connect this to the yellow block with the green flag. Click on the number below the arrow and change it to 10.

When you press the green flag at the top of the screen, your "L" should drop into place.

5. Transfer File to Students.

Once the file is set up, the next step is to transfer it to students. Click on the yellow box in the extreme upper right of the screen. Name your project, and then click share by e-mail. You will be prompted to answer a simple math problem, which passes as proof of adult supervision. E-mail the file directly to your students' devices.

On each device, open the e-mail and download the file. Once it completes downloading, press the "open in" button and select the ScratchJr app. The file should then open within the app, ready for students to begin.

6. Set Up Guided Access.

On each device, triple-click the home button to activate Guided Access mode and confirm that you have turned off the desired part of the screen. The first time you set up Guided Access, it will take a couple of minutes per device, but thereafter, when you turn on Guided Access, it launches the last setup you used. If you just use Guided Access for programming lessons you have created in ScratchJr, it will deploy quickly.

7. Record Demonstration Video.

Using a screen capture program, record a quick video explaining how to program the letters onto the line. Include turning on the grid button to make it easy for the students to count how many spaces the letter has to move. When you talk about moving the letter, highlight the math by asking, "If we begin at 13 and end at 3, how many spaces will we move?" and "What is the difference between 13 and 3?" Show this video at the beginning of class, but also make a copy available to the students as they work, in case they need to see it again.

CURRICULUM MAP FOR LITERACY
LESSONS IN SCRATCHJR K-2

Each of the lessons in this sequence builds upon those previous, in complexity of literacy task as well as programming challenge. These lessons would just be a couple in the entire school year, but clearly there is a progression in complexity.

Table 9.1   Literacy in ScratchJr, Scope and Sequence

Grade	Lesson Description	Literacy Learning Objective
Kindergarten	Match letters and animals	Initial sound awareness
Kindergarten/first	Single sight words and first names	Spelling sight words
First	Sight word families	Spelling sight words
First	Word ladders	Understanding relationship between words
First/second	Words into simple sentences with punctuation	Syntax
Second	Dialogue construction	Writing dialogues

Match Letters with Animals

In this kindergarten lesson, include animals as well their initial letters as sprites. So for example, a fish, a cat, and the letters F and C. The students program the animal to walk to the correct letter.

This lesson can extend further into literacy by adding more letters and animals, and include the ending sounds of the animals' names.

This lesson can be extended further into programming by adding the yellow "sprite touch" event trigger in place of the green flag. The icon is two figures facing each other touching hands. This allows students to write a program that becomes active when one sprite touches another. This is the perfect trigger to make the animal dance once it reaches its letter.

Single Sight Words and First Names

This kindergarten level lesson is detailed in the step-by-step directions above. You can build on the single word lesson by adding more levels by adding scenes. To add a scene, press the plus sign in the right-hand column. This adds backgrounds. Be sure to add a line to each background. Each level can be a classmate's name. This also works well as a paired programming activity.

Sight Word Families

Building on the single sight word lesson, for this first-grade appropriate activity, you are going to take a group of related sight words (the, they, there, then) and create a sprite for each letter (e, e, h, n, r, t, y). The students have to identify a sight word from the jumbled letters and then program the letters onto the line. This is a classic word jumble with a sequencing upgrade.

This lesson can be extended by adding more word families in more scenes, becoming a multileveled experience. This lesson can be extended into more complex programming by becoming word ladders. An extension of this activity would be to have students create their own levels and then share them with each other. The students could play and respond to each other's levels.

Building their own levels requires students to look at a family of sight words, break them down into letters, and then reassemble them. This is a lesson where you can see the word wall paying dividends in real time. During this activity, I would have students working in pairs to support content-rich conversations about which word family to choose. The decision about which letters are needed requires close analysis of the entire word family, and the amazing thing is that during most of this time, the students will think that they are focused primarily on the programming platform's mechanics or appearance.

Truth be told, this activity would be great on a desktop with letter tiles. The conversations about spelling would be no less meaningful. This is the mark of a great lesson that uses tech: the tech supports what would be a good idea without the tech. By adding programming, we cash in on the logic-building benefits of sequencing and programming.

Word Ladders

A word ladder is when you begin with one word and see how many different words you can make by only changing one letter at a time. The previous lesson is a great foundation for this activity, because in this lesson the challenge is the programming. To get a word ladder to work, students have to use the orange wait block.

The wait block is orange and has a stopwatch icon on it. In programming, wait blocks are used to control the sequence of events. The larger the number you place in the wait block, the longer it will wait. In the word ladder, a student might begin with the word "There" and wants the second word to be "Here." The student will add a wait block to every letter except T. The student will program T to leave the line, and "Here" will wait behind.

If the students work at this step by step, they can actually create some amazing sequences of words and actions.

Words into Simple Sentences with Punctuation

In this first- and second-grade level adaptation of the single sight word lesson, the teacher creates sprites that are words and punctuation. The students have to program the words into the right order to create a sentence. The focus of this lesson is syntax, which is well supported by the content as well as the act of programming. The sentence could be "The red cat danced." The lesson could then be extended further into programming by asking the students to make a red cat dance.

Dialogue Construction

This lesson is not built on the single sight word model, but instead asks students to create a short animation based on something they are learning about. Building on decades of successful "write a skit about X" assignments, this programming lesson asks students to create an animated dialogue in ScratchJr.

The programming challenge in this lesson is the use of messages. The most powerful of the yellow event blocks, messages, allow you to place a trigger at the end of a program. In a dialogue, this is a great tool because programming with wait blocks gets really hard. The students can write a program where one sprite asks a question, and then the program sends a message to the other character to trigger the response to the question.

Students can make the characters speak by either using the speech bubbles (purple) or the live recording blocks (green).

Chapter 10

Programming to Learn in Elementary STEM

STEM in elementary education is a golden invitation for kids to mix stuff together, make a mess, and learn about how the world works by working with the world. STEM stands for Science, Technology, Engineering, and Mathematics and, in this context, means an integrated hands-on approach to science in grades K-5. There are a few ways that programming can support students learning in STEM and even make that learning visible and shareable.

A great STEM lesson has something in it that students can discover. In most cases, the joy of discovery is not happening behind the screen of an iPad. While there are likely hundreds of great ways programming in elementary grades can be a meaningful part of the STEM curriculum, in this chapter we will discuss how robots can be used as experimental tools and how students can use programming to design interactive models and presentations of scientific systems.

Discovery-Based Learning

Earlier in the book we discussed lesson design with robots and the various roles a robot can play in a lesson. For elementary STEM learning, the most useful role is robot-as-constant. In one example of this lesson type, second grade students were using a Sphero robot programmed in the Tickle app to explore inclined planes and learn their properties.

The room was prepared with seven different ramps employing a variety of pitch and length combinations. Each pair of students got a Sphero that was programmed to roll forward for five seconds at fifty percent power. The students were not allowed to alter the program at this point. The lesson was introduced not by a discussion of inclined planes, but with a discussion of a constant and how two things can be compared through the use of a constant.

After the students understood that in this experiment the constant was the robot, we set them loose to explore the selection of ramps.

In this lesson, the students were given the choice of which station they wanted to start at and even the choice of when to move from one station to another. This worked well in this lesson, as the stations could accommodate many robots each, and the stations were not drastically different from one another. The stations were of equal interest and play value, and each pair of students had a small whiteboard that they could use as an inclined plane. Overall, there were many more ramps than robots in the room, and no students were standing around holding their robots waiting for a free ramp.

After just ten minutes of exploration, robots were stopped, and students reported on what they had learned about inclined planes. As students talked, the teacher made notes and charts on the board. There was no front-loading of information about inclined planes; instead, here in the middle of the lesson, the students share what they notice, and the teacher collects impressions into facts about inclined planes.

Programming almost didn't play a part in this lesson; in fact, the lesson as described only had the teacher programming. The second graders were using a tool that was programmed by the teacher. After the share-out of discoveries, the students were allowed to program the Sphero differently if they wanted to, and some did; others continued to explore the various ramps.

If the lesson were extended to include programming the robot, recording observations, and then changing the robot's program, there would be a functional need for students to program. As students get more comfortable with programming platforms, you will be able to ask them to do more in those platforms.

The Power of Interactive Animations

Programming is a transformational educational tool because it allows teachers and students to communicate in ways never before possible. Before programming to learn, when students wanted to describe how a system works—for instance, why an eclipse happens—they were challenged to show the multiple components in each system and to describe and demonstrate how those parts interrelate. With open studio platforms like Scratch, Tynker, and ScratchJr, students of all ages can program an animated model of a system to demonstrate and develop their own understanding.

When fifth grade is learning about eclipses, one easy support activity is to use Hopscotch or another open studio platform to program the Sun, the Moon, and the Earth orbiting each other. As students watch their own model, they should notice how often an eclipse forms. Can they predict when the next one will happen? As students work on these models, have them share with each other. Once students share their model and see the models others have built, they often return to their own model to make changes and incorporate ideas.

When students work together, they are developing their own understanding with their classmates. This allows students to explore and learn while still ending at the correct understanding of the concept. The models students can build in a programming platform only need to be good enough to support a conversation about an idea. Students in first grade can program a coral reef, and while it may not look like a real coral reef, they build real understanding in the process of completing the project.

Building Our Understanding

The LEGO WeDo kits offer a science and STEM curriculum that puts building at the center of the learning experience. Through building an amusement park and a construction site, students explore physics fundamentals. This is a very visual application of programming and building, putting the T and E in STEM front and center. The LEGO curriculum pack is well developed and contains instructions for teachers on implementation and planning.

As with any packaged curriculum, teachers thinking about implementing STEM with LEGO WeDo should look closely at the provided lessons and figure out how the activities support the current grade-level learning goals. Teaching with LEGO can be a logistical challenge; the materials available for purchase from LEGO can make it easier, but be mindful of the prep and pieces needed.

The strength of the amusement park and construction zone projects is that there are multiple components to each project. Small groups of students can build the components separately and then explore them all together. The LEGO projects serve as a model of a lesson centered on an experience more than an idea. The challenge as a teacher is to make the building meaningful for all students involved.

Like many things in the STEM marketplace, the teacher has to evaluate what experience the tool can help students access. The teacher has to build a learning experience that is much bigger than supplying students with materials and a set of directions. Are we playing with LEGO and robots and pretending it is learning, or has a goal been set, supported, and assessed?

Permission to Play

We can play and learn important lessons. When teachers understand the tools and can build the needed supports, all students can use connected toys and learning tools to program their way to an increased understanding of STEM. When teachers carefully construct the context, play is exploration. Running the robot over every ramp, students discover which ramps allow the robot to roll the farthest and the fastest. This observation, when shared with the group, grows into knowledge the group owns. When we guide students through learning by discovery, we are teaching them how to learn about their world.

Sphero robots have discovery-based learning at the center of their mission, so it isn't surprising that their lessons can serve as guide for good tech integration into STEM. For the K-5 age group, Sphero has some core lessons and STEM challenges that can be adapted to work with younger students. Most of the activities are designed for fourth and fifth grades but, with instruction and support, can be successful with younger students.

Whether the challenge is designing a boat that the robot can propel or using it to unravel the mysteries of rate, time, and distance, these hands-on activities get students working together, collecting data, and drawing conclusions. The playful nature of the tool helps them relax and have fun as they work together. Even if the lessons are not a great match for your students, looking closely at the resources on Sphero's SPRK website can help guide decisions made about tech integration towards playful, hands-on solutions.

Making Learning Interactive

The design process and physical building can easily be components of a great STEM lesson. The Makey Makey interface allows students to build physical interfaces to interact with. On the simplest level they might build a piano out of bananas, but students can also create their own games and challenges that have a physical aspect as well as a programmed aspect.

There is a great Makey Makey community online, and Josh Burker's book *The Invent To Learn Guide To Fun* provides powerful, detailed instructions on using Makey Makey and other amazing tools in the classroom.

Chapter 11

Resources and Quick-Start Lesson Ideas

There are a bunch of great resources out there about programming, and more are developed all the time. Let this list be a starting point. Be sure to check BeyondtheHourofCode.com for additional resources and screenshots of some of the quick-start lessons.

RESOURCES

One of the greatest resources available to you is the knowledge of your students. Nothing supplants that, and it is the shaping factor teachers must bring to every lesson they plan and every tool they adopt. No matter what has been built, the teacher brings it into the class space and manages the translation to students.

The second most valuable resource is the past. The Apple II computer came out in 1977, and teachers have been trying to use programming in schools since then. The technology has become more mobile and easier to place into a variety of learning contexts. We are no longer trapped in a computer lab stuck behind a monitor. Look to the early work of teachers using LOGO in the classroom. They created art and design projects and interactive games. There are hundreds of great ideas just waiting for an update in these instructional libraries.

Websites and Organizations

Code.org is dedicated to bringing computer science into every classroom. The resources they have collected on this site are legion. There is a programming solution for almost any age and tech access combination imaginable. The web-based programming tools on the site can support many of the lessons discussed in this book. Any teacher or administrator interested in bringing programming to their school or classroom should employ the deep resources sponsored by Code.org. Each year, Code.org hosts free in-person professional development workshops in many different locations to support programming adoption in schools.

The Computer Science Teachers Association (http://www.csta.acm.org/) has been supporting computer science education since 2005. The resources curated here can help teachers find training and support materials or other teachers to connect with. While the mission of this book is to help programming reach beyond computer science learning goals, some of the best partners in this process are computer science teachers who know programming well.

Awesome People to Follow

Vicky Sedgwick (@VisionsbyVicky) is a K-8 technology instructor at a school in Southern California. She is an active member of the twitter communities at #csk8 as well as #kidscancode. Vicky blogs occasionally at http://vsedgwick.edublogs.org/, and she always shares great new tools. Vicky is a great teacher to know online, because she is always willing to answer a question or to help locate a resource. Vicky helped a great deal with this book, and many of the ideas presented here bear the mark of her influence.

Brian Briggs (@Bribriggs) is the director of innovation and technology for Plumas Lake School District. He is pioneering the use of robots and drones in education. He is also on the cutting edge of all things Kickstarter. If you want a clear perspective on something brand new to the tech scene, check out Brian's Twitter feed.

David Saunders (@DesignSaunders) is a librarian and image of the makerspace at a school in Connecticut. David is an innovator with a keen eye to engagement and invention. His past projects include building a Shakespeare version of Zoltar from the movie *Big*. David knows a great deal about tinkering in education, especially using littleBits and Raspberry Pi computers to help students design working prototypes. Be sure to read more at his blog http://designsaunders.com/.

Jen Gilbert (@msgilbertrocks) is a teacher passionate about technology and programming to learn. She shares her adventures on Twitter and Instagram as well as her blog http://www.msgilbertrocks.com/. Jen is a regular and thoughtful contributor to the #kidscancode and #csk8 discussions on Twitter, and she models a passion for learning new things and figuring out how they best fit into the classroom.

Grant Hosford (@codesparkceo) is the CEO and co-founder of codeSpark, a venture backed learning game company turning programming into play for young kids. The LEGO Foundation recently honored codeSpark as one of thirty global companies "Re-imagining Learning." The son of educators, Grant, is a passionate advocate for getting more girls and minorities interested in STEM careers.

QUICK-START LESSONS

These are not the best plans in the world, just the quickest. Try them out. They are outlined here in a way to make adaption easy.

Sphero Quick Lessons

Before your students can discover the fundamentals of physics, calculus, and time travel with the Sphero robot, they have to be able to make it go where they need it to go. These simple lessons require very little prep and give the students just enough structure to sustain engagement.

1. Aim Is the Game: In each of these activities, ask your students to pair the Sphero every time they switch users. This will get them comfortable with the calibration interface, and it will also get them in the habit of aiming early and often. (Pairing is connecting the tablet's Bluetooth to the robots. Aiming is when the user and the spherical robot come to an agreement about with direction is zero degree.)
2. From Here to There: A great starting activity is to just put some points on the floor and ask the students to drive from one to the other. First allow them to follow the robot while driving from point A to point B and back again. The second time they drive the route, they have to stand at point A and drive to B and back. It is HARD to drive the robot when it is coming toward you, giving them playful practice.
3. I Walk the Line: Using masking tape, mark several lanes on the floor of your room. Ask students to use either the Sphero Drive app, Draw N' Drive, SPRK, or Tickle to drive the lane. Encourage experimentation. What do they learn about how to best control the Sphero?
4. The Obstacle Course: Create a course in the classroom where the students will have to program the Sphero to travel from start to finish without knocking over objects that are spread out through the course. To build coding skills, students should navigate the maze using the SPRK, Tickle, Macrolab, or Tynker apps. This is best done in teams, so that students can communicate as they create their code. If it doesn't work, team members can go back and edit their code. As they get better at navigating the course, you can make it more creative and complex for the students. Eventually,

ask the students to create their own obstacle courses and challenge each
other.

5. Bocce Ball: Like Bocce Ball? Substitute Bocce Balls with Spheros, and
set up a game where students program their Sphero to roll down the lane
and stop on a small target. This activity works very well with the Draw
N' Drive app, but SPRK, Macrolab, Tickle, or Tynker could be used to
program Sphero for this activity. The other team then has the opportunity
to write some code to either get their ball closer to the target or else knock
the other team's Sphero farther away. Other teachers have done something
similar, adapting the Spheros to create their own bowling game. Both
games are fun and engaging ways to program the robotic balls, while supporting communication and problem solving.

ScratchJr Quick Lessons

ScratchJr is the best tablet-based programming app for prereaders of all time.
Getting students to the point where they are ScratchJr-comfortable only takes
a lesson or two.

1. Scratch the Dancing Cat: Two of the most important things students need
to know are how to begin a program and how to tell the sprite to move.
This lesson hits both of those points. The challenge for students is to
design an awesome dance for Scratch the cat. To create a dance, they will
need to use the green flag event block (this triggers the program to begin
when the green flag is clicked) combined with several of the blue movement pieces. Students can work in pairs to create a crazy dance. While
they create the dance, they will discover many other commands in the
app. This is discovery-based learning. Teachers create the conditions for
learning by putting the student in the learning experience. When students
share something they have learned, their teachers and classmates are an
active and engaged audience.

2. Make an Aquarium: Building on the prior lesson focused on movement,
the aquarium lesson uses movement complemented by loop blocks. There
are two different types of loops. In this lesson, students figure out how
to use them both to create a scene that goes on for a long time. Students
will add characters in this lesson and may even figure out how to edit
and recolor the characters. This lesson is a very simple version of using
programming to model behavior. The science would be much better if the
students watched an aquarium and then modeled one.

3. Tell a Story: Read a story as a class, and ask the students to retell or extend
the narrative based on your needs. If the students have not found the record
sound block by this lesson, please clue them in. Ask them to use the record

sound block to record themselves narrating parts of the story the sprites on-screen are acting out.

4. Say Cheese: Have the students put themselves in the program using the sprite edit function and the camera import. Students can make a classroom scene by using the camera to create a classroom background and then placing themselves in the action, adding their own faces to the stock characters. This lesson is very fun for the students, but it is building an important skill. Once students are comfortable using the camera to bring class content into the app, they can program about anything they are learning. Worksheets can be imported into ScratchJr, and more meaningful answers can be programmed.

Dash and Dot Fast Launch

The only thing that is going to slow down an awesome lesson with Dash and Dot is if the students have never used them before. Here are a quick series of microlessons that will get kids familiar with the cutest educational robots on the shelves.

1. Go Dash Go!: Drive Dash around the room using the remote control. Have the students work in small groups to discover and record what each control on the Go app does. Finish the lesson by having each group teach the class two things about the Go app. The greatest thing about this structure is that it requires students to create and share knowledge. This type of lesson develops your classroom as a knowledge community.

2. I Like to Move It, Move It: Using Blockly, get Dash navigating the room. Place Dot some distance from Dash, and ask students to program Dash to find Dot. In addition, ask the students to use the robots' sensing capabilities to have Dash and Dot both celebrate when they find each other. Be sure to remind your students that a good celebration includes a light show, always.

3. Action and Reaction: Using both robots programmed in Blockly, the students have to make Dot laugh when Dash wakes her up. There are several ways to do this, and it might not take a long time. This type of small-scope discovery challenge is great for building a better understanding of the possibilities of programming as well as the mechanics of the interface.

4. Robot Joust: In this design challenge, students build armor for Dash and program him to "joust" by arranging specific targets that are marked on the floor with tape or built out of wood blocks.

5. Reunion: Using the Tickle app, program Dash and Dot to light up when they see each other, and then film a scene where they are reunited after a long absence.

Station Activities for Hopscotch

1. Art Bot: Using the draw loop programming elements, the students create amazing multicolored artworks. Be sure to have a blog, or at least a shared screen, so all students can show off their creations. If your students are working on their own device, encourage them to screenshot their art and install it as a wallpaper on their device. You could also suggest that they e-mail it home for their parent or guardian to use as a wallpaper on their device. The phone is the new fridge. As a station, this is a good short activity, and students can work in pairs or individually.

2. Discovering Regular Polygons: Once students know the program for drawing a square, they can figure out how to draw many other shapes. This station would have an instructional video reminding students how to use loops and rotations in Hopscotch to create regular polygons. The code for a square would be provided, and the students would have a T-Chart with other rows blank or only partly filled out. Each student at this station would be challenged to figure out as many polygons as possible and program them in to prove they work. As students challenge themselves to use more sides, the shapes slowly approach a circle.

3. Study a Game: In this lesson, you will ask students to find a game they like to play in the Hopscotch community. Set a time limit on selection. Once the student(s) decide on a game, ask them to remix or branch from that game and learn something about how the game works. As students work, have them share out lessons. This lesson can be streamlined by identifying the game element or mechanic that you want them to learn more about. This is the programming equivalent to taking apart the alarm clock. It might not work when the students are done, but they will know more about it than when they began.

4. The Power of <3: Hopscotch has an amazing function: characters can be added from the emoji keyboard. Challenge the students to figure out how to make roses or hearts or devils dance across the screen, get big, or disappear completely when they run into each other. Be sure you take a good look at ALL the characters in the emoji keyboard before telling your students about it.

Station Activities for Tickle

Tickle is a great Blockly-based programming app that connects to robots and other Internet-enabled things. In the classroom using Tickle to drive a Sphero, Ollie, or Dash robot makes it possible to move programming off of the screen and into the real world. In Hopscotch, the sprites on the screen leave a colored line behind them, and, thanks to some masking tape and a marker, so does Dash.

1. Get Moving: Using a sprite inside the app or a robot of your choice, have the students use the movement blocks in Tickle to get something moving. If it is on the screen, set up a series of waypoints. If students are steering robots, start by just asking them to go from point A to point B and back.
2. Drawing Challenge: Leave markers, tape, string, clay, and other supplies at this station, along with the Dash robot and some paper. Ask the students to design a way for Dash to hold the marker and program Dash to draw a shape. Each group hangs their drawing on the wall before rotating to the next station. The group with the best drawing (as judged by the class) could give a short explanation of how they attached the marker to the robot and how they wrote their program.
3. Puzzle Bot: In this challenge, the students have a Sphero in a box. There is one hole in the box that is slightly larger than the Sphero. The students have to write a program in Tickle that "solves" the puzzle of the box. If your students get good at this, add walls and alleys inside the box. This creates a type of blind labyrinth.

Lesson One: Kodable

Start Kodable with the off-line activity of Fuzz Family Frenzy. It is available on the Code.org website as well as Kodable.com. This off-line activity asks students to program each other to navigate through a simple obstacle course. After this activity is complete, pair the students on an iPad. Have them play level one, interacting with the tutorial. The challenge for teachers is not to interfere with the tutorial.

The tutorial is showing the students how the app operates, but it has a more important function. The tutorial helps the students understand that there is a knowledge resource in the app. The interface has something to teach the students. Until the students understand that there is knowledge somewhere other than in the teacher's head, they will look nowhere else. If the teacher runs through the tutorial, then the teacher represents themselves as the authority.

Ask students to share their discoveries as they work. Whether the room is bubbling with triumph or roiling with discovery-yet-to-happen, a good focused and short verbal reporting-out can help students understand their own experience of learning in a much broader context.

Lesson One: The Foos

If the students in your class have done any coding in any app ever, just put them in pairs and get them into The Foos. Have the students identify the goal of the level before they begin to program. The Foos has a good tutorial as well. Once the students are through the tutorial level, create situations where students can share their knowledge and understanding of the game with each other. Don't neglect this opportunity to build the knowledge community in your classroom.

At the end of each group of challenges in The Foos, there is a playground area where students can have the characters do anything. In this way, The Foos has a foot in both the world of leveled apps and the world of open studio apps.

Teachers looking for a more supported introduction to The Foos can use the lessons provided on their Hour of Code page at http://www.thefoos.com/hourofcode/.

Acknowledgments

This book was a collaboration on so many levels. On the closest level, it would never have been possible if my wife Melissa had not encouraged and supported me. I am grateful to the amazing teachers I work with everyday, who let me into their classrooms and kindly smile when I change their plans for them. Thank you, Sally, Tali, Morgan, Donna, Danielle, Megan, Stacy, Diane, Heather, Vicky, Lauren, Stacey, Anne, Candace, Elizabeth, Amy, and Hilary.

In addition to my local support, I was fortunate enough to have a squad of volunteer readers. Thank you to my beta readers, especially Vicky Sedgwick, Michelle Tolub, Jen Gilbert, Axel Reitzig, and Michelle Eckstein. Without the dedicated work of Fred Burke, this book would not be fit to read. Thank you.

Index

About the Author

Sam Patterson, MFA, EdD, has been teaching for sixteen years and is currently a technology integration specialist at the Gideon Hausner Jewish Day School in Palo Alto, California. Sam loves working with elementary teachers to discover new ways that technology can support progressive pedagogy and student empowerment. Sam brings a background of poetry and literacy studies to the tech lessons he designs with the teachers at his school. He blogs for Edutopia.org, MyPaperlessClassroom.com, and is a cohost of the TechEducator Podcast.

Programming in the
Primary Grades